Motorbooks  Illustrated Buyer's Guide Series

Illustrated

JOHN DEERE
TWO-CYLINDER TRACTOR
BUYER'S ★ GUIDE™

Robert N. Pripps
Foreword by Jack Cherry, Two-Cylinder Club

Motorbooks International
Publishers & Wholesalers ®

To Douglas, my number three son;
his appreciation for the old ways has led him
to become a pretty fair amateur blacksmith.

First published in 1992 by Motorbooks
International Publishers & Wholesalers, PO Box
2, 729 Prospect Avenue, Osceola, WI 54020 USA

© Robert N. Pripps, 1992

Motorbooks International is a certified
trademark, registered with the United States
Patent Office

The information in this book is true and complete
to the best of our knowledge. All
recommendations are made without any
guarantee on the part of the author or Publisher,
who also disclaim any liability incurred in
connection with the use of this data or specific
details

We recognize that some words, model names and
designations, for example, mentioned herein are
the property of the trademark holder. We use
them for identification purposes only. This is not
an official publication

Motorbooks International books are also available
at discounts in bulk quantity for industrial or
sales-promotional use. For details write to Special
Sales Manager at the Publisher's address

Library of Congress Cataloging-in-Publication
Data
Pripps, Robert N.
     Illustrated John Deere two-cylinder tractor
buyer's guide / Robert N. Pripps.
        p.   cm.—(Motorbooks International
illustrated buyer's guide series)
     Includes index and bibliographical
references.
     ISBN 0-87938-659-2
     1. John Deere tractors—Collectors and
collecting.   2. John Deere tractors—
Purchasing.   I. Deere & Company.   II. Title.
III. Series.
TL233.5.P76   1992
629.225—dc20   92-19207

On the front cover: The classic, unstyled John
Deere Model A two-cylinder general-purpose
row-crop tractor with a wide-tread front end and
rubber tires. *Andrew Morland*

Printed and bound in the United States of
America

Contents

Acknowledgments

A nice pair of regulars, a D and a BR (Regular, or Standard-Tread). Both are 1937 models owned by L. Walgenlock of Oglesby, Illinois. The tractors were called regulars, or standard-treads, because the wheel width spacing could not be changed.

I thank the following:

Ralph C. Hughes, director of Advertising, Deere & Company, and Donald S. Huber, manager of Creative Services, Deere & Company, who provided help, encouragement, photographs, and information.

Dr. Buryl McFadden, engine scientist with the US Air Force, farmer, and John Deere collector, for providing technical information and a contagious high regard for John Deere tractors and equipment.

Artistic Photo Lab, Rockford, Illinois, for the special attention to detail in developing my photos.

Jack Cherry, editor of *Two-Cylinder* magazine, for help and advice and for taking time from his busy schedule to write the foreword to this book.

Les Stegh, archivist with the Deere Library and Record Retention Department, for help with serial numbers, prices, and old pictures.

Michael Dregni, editor, and the staff at Motorbooks International, for pulling all this material together and making it look good.

Foreword

By Jack Cherry

By the time I had gotten into the meat of the *Illustrated John Deere Two-Cylinder Tractor Buyer's Guide* manuscript as the book was being prepared, it had already become obvious that Robert Pripps was taking an entirely new approach in evaluating the collectibility of John Deere two-cylinder tractors. Having started as a novice on the subject, but blessed with a technical background, he traveled a different avenue of logic to set things straight in his own mind.

The result is a new method of tractor evaluation that can be used by anyone, and it's a guide that will undoubtedly become widely accepted by collectors. The "family line" arrangement of tractors is a departure from the typical chronological method, and when combined with the star rating system, it's not only easy to visualize and remember, but will probably serve as the basis for evaluation standardization in this field.

If any part of the guide is likely to be controversial, it's the assignment of specific star ratings on various tractors. Some collectors might suggest increasing or reducing the number of stars for a certain model—even to the point of rationalizing that if some fairly late standard-treads rate a five, then surely a Model C should get a six. That's tough to do with a five-star system.

As with any new system with multiple interrelated facets, probably some refinements will be necessary in years to come to maintain perspective with future experience. Indeed, changes in the sport of two-cylinder collecting itself will likely be the cause of the greatest number of rating changes. As the extremely rare models become permanent additions in collections, the next tier will take their place in the five-star rankings. To stay with the same example, who would have thought, just a few years ago, that some late-model standard-treads would be among the most desirable today?

Regardless of the reader's personal feelings with the ratings, let it be known that after immersing himself in the study of John Deere two-cylinder tractors, Mr. Pripps became firmly convinced that none rated less than two stars. That, in itself, is a great compliment to the judgment of all who are involved in this grand adventure.

Jack Cherry
Editor, *Two-Cylinder* magazine

Introduction

When Michael Dregni, editor at Motorbooks, suggested a John Deere two-cylinder buyer's guide to me, he sent me several samples of other buyer's guides published by Motor- books. One of these was for Indian motorcycles. Now, Michael is a motorcycle enthusiast and a collector and restorer of old motorcycles, so he suggested to me that I try to

A 1937 Model BR. Regulars were considered plowing tractors, being lower and heavier than the GPs. Thus, they were popular in wheat country.

reflect, in this John Deere book, the "passion" that is evidenced in the Indian book.

Well, being basically a technical man, I cannot say whether or not the reader will sense passion in these pages, but I will say that in the course of researching and writing this book, my regard for the mighty two-cylinder has greatly increased over that which I had before, and that was a lot. It truly is a unique type of machine that seems—at least to me and to several thousand other two-cylinder collectors—to represent the finest of American ingenuity and integrity. The green and yellow John Deere did, and does, symbolize the self-reliant, determined, and capable American farmers, who, though often penalized for their productivity, have fed the United States and much of the world.

Whether or not this book achieves Michael's goals for passion, my John Deere cap is off to Deere & Company for making these great tractors from 1914 to 1960—and, I understand, even better ones today—and to the American farmer, and to the collectors and restorers who are keeping this legacy alive.

This book is intended to help the collector or potential collector choose a tractor. The star rating system should be helpful when considering the investment potential of a tractor. The number of stars assigned is based on uniqueness, availability, and desirability. Also appearing in this book is a classification system for the condition of a tractor. Use of these systems should be helpful in both advertising a tractor for sale and describing one over the phone.

Horsepowers specified in this book are the maximums listed in the Nebraska Tractor Test ratings. They are not always consistent with Deere figures, since Deere, in its conservative way, usually listed a "continuous" rating, which was lower.

The Deere history is so long—over 150 years—and the tractor product line so broad that I couldn't put all available data in this

A 1936 Model BW. Note the round-spoke wheels.

book. The "Recommended Reading" and "Sources" sections at the end of the book will provide places where other specific data can be obtained.

This book is arranged along model family lines, rather than just chronologically, as most John Deere tractor books are. This should help you to get the data on the specific model that interests you.

Enjoy!

My 1948 John Deere Model B at work under the guiding hand of grandson Tyler, age eight, while I empty maple sap into the hauling tank. The hand clutch, a high-torque engine, and creeper gears make Deere tractors such as this easier for young ones to drive.

Chapter 1

The John Deere Family

Between 1914 and 1960, Deere & Company —and the company it acquired in 1918, the Waterloo Gasoline Engine Company—produced a family of two-cylinder tractors, renowned for their dependability, ease of maintenance, and durability. Initially, they were designed to lift the burden of farming from human and horse power and place it on horsepower—that is, the mechanical power of the tractor. As might well be expected, this was an evolutionary, not revolutionary, prospect.

Evolution of the Product Line

The initial tasks of the tractor were, in the main, driving the threshing machine and plowing. The first of the line of tractors, the Waterloo Boy, was essentially a stationary engine mounted on a running gear. It was designed to emulate the steam traction engine but with internal combustion.

Later, as disk harrowing, dragging, and general pulling were added to the tractor's tasks, an awareness of the need for improved maneuverability came about. Thus, a shorter, more manageable version, the Model D, evolved.

Finally, the general-purpose tractor made the Deere scene in the form of the Model GP, or General Purpose, with four means of power output: traction, belt, power takeoff (PTO), and power implement lift. The GP was the first of the long line of row-crop tractors to follow.

This did not mean that the squat standard-tread tractors disappeared, however. Although they did not enjoy the popularity of the row-crops, they were an important part of the family. First, in the thirties, came the lettered series, following the example of the Model D; then came the two-number series; and finally came the three-number series.

With each successive progression, the horse was further replaced by the more

The Model BO Lindeman, a crawler modification of an orchard version of the B. This version was mostly used in the orchards of the American West, where the tracks provided the needed traction and stability for the steep hillsides. The Lindeman firm did the crawler modification to the Deere tractor. Lindeman was based in Yakima, Washington.

The famous Waterloo Boy Kerosene-Burning Tractor—forerunner of the first John Deere Tractor. Taken over by John Deere in 1918.

The John Deere Model D of 1924—the distillate-burning tractor that set a new standard for simplicity, economy, and dependability.

The present Model D . . . the greatest of all Model D's in economy, in performance, in VALUE.

The highly-refined John Deere Model A General Purpose Tractor—a combination of simplicity, light weight, compact construction, speed, economy, and adaptability.

Built low to get under the low-hanging branches and with streamlined hood John Deere Orchard Tractors are making friends among fruit growers everywhere.

A Brief History of
JOHN DEERE *Two Cylinder* Tractors

ALTHOUGH the greatest progress in the perfection of the farm tractor has been made since the World War, tractors were actually being used on farms during the "Gay Nineties".

On August 15, 1892, a single-cylinder, gasoline-burning tractor engine, built by John Froelich, of Girard, Iowa, was put into service near Langford, South Dakota.

This outfit was truly a tractor—something new in its day; for it not only supplied power for belt work, but it could actually move itself and pull other machinery at the same time.

Forerunner of John Deere

Between John Froelich's pioneer gas tractor engine of 1892 and the modern John Deere tractors of today, there is a direct chain of events in manufacturing history.

On January 10, 1893, a number of business men of Waterloo, Iowa, joined with Mr. Froelich in organizing the Waterloo Gasoline Traction Engine Company for the purpose of developing the manufacture of the Froelich tractor.

"Waterloo Boy" Introduced

In 1896, this concern was organized as the Waterloo Gasoline Engine Company. It achieved great success in building gasoline engines and continued painstaking experimental work with tractors, confident that the future would bring a great farm demand for them. In 1912, it brought out the successful Waterloo Boy Kerosene-Burning Tractor.

In March, 1918, the Waterloo Gasoline Engine Company was purchased by Deere & Company, and tractor development became the main business of the factory that had pioneered in the building of tractors.

Two Cylinders Most Economical

The goal of the factory, under the ownership and operation of Deere & Company, was the development of a practical tractor that could be operated by the average farmer at the lowest possible cost. Careful experiments were conducted with many types of tractors. Results indicated clearly that the two-cylinder type of tractor, by proper designing, could be best adapted to meet the farmers' requirements.

In 1924, the John Deere Model D Two-Cylinder Tractor was put on the market. Its success has been tremendous from the beginning. Farmers have welcomed it because it gives them a combination of features outstanding in the tractor field—great power, light weight, extreme simplicity, ease of adjustment and operation, plus the most important thing of all—low operating costs.

First General Purpose Model in 1928

The popular John Deere General Purpose Standard-Tread Tractor was introduced during the season of 1928. This was the first tractor of any make to be equipped with a power lift. It found an immediate welcome from farmers who had been wanting a tractor similar to the Model D, but a tractor that would do all-around farm work including planting and cultivating. This tractor was also produced in an orchard model, with low chassis and seat and shielded wheels.

The first John Deere General Purpose Tractor with adjustable tread (the Model A) was introduced in the fall of 1934, and the new Model B General Purpose, smaller brother of the Model A, was first offered to farmers in all sections of the country in the spring of 1935.

Since then, many other models of John Deere Tractors have followed the Model B in rapid succession—the Models AR and BR Standard Tread Tractors, the Models AO and BO Orchard Tractors, the Models AN and BN with single front wheels, and the Models AW and BW with adjustable tread in front as well as in rear.

Thus, the complete line of John Deere Tractors for farm use, now consists of eleven models—a size and type for every farm.

Outline of the John Deere two-cylinder tractor's history from the John Deere *Power Farming With Greater Profit* pamphlet produced in 1937 by Deere & Co. to celebrate its centennial and promote its future. *Deere & Company*

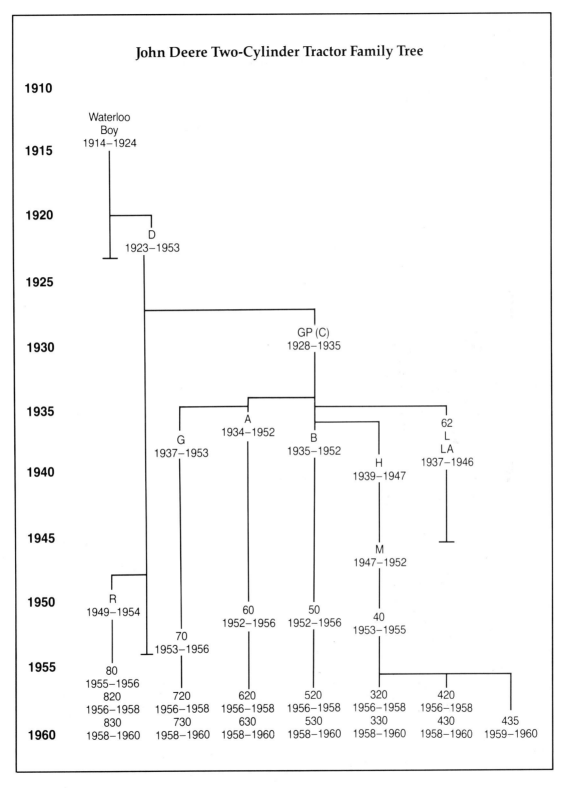

John Deere Two-Cylinder Tractor Family Tree

1910

1915   Waterloo Boy 1914–1924

1920   D 1923–1953

1925

1930   GP (C) 1928–1935

1935   A 1934–1952   B 1935–1952   62 L LA 1937–1946

   G 1937–1953   H 1939–1947

1940

1945   M 1947–1952

1950   R 1949–1954   60 1952–1956   50 1952–1956   40 1953–1955

   70 1953–1956

1955

80 1955–1956						
820 1956–1958	720 1956–1958	620 1956–1958	520 1956–1958	320 1956–1958	420 1956–1958	
830 1958–1960	730 1958–1960	630 1958–1960	530 1958–1960	330 1958–1960	430 1958–1960	435 1959–1960

1960

economical tractor. Note that each horse consumed the produce of two acres of land each year. This was a considerable burden to the farmer, especially the farmer with few acres.

By the early forties, only the stubborn, or those whose religion dictated animal power, were still defending the horse as a source of routine farm power. The intervention of World War II, however, delayed horse replacement. After the war, the drive for improvement in the John Deere line came more from advancing farm technology than from competition with the horse.

The two-cylinder family consisted of six or seven basic sizes of tractors, each aimed at filling an agricultural requirement. Many of the size models were subdivided into variations with characteristics particularly suited to certain types of farms. Thus arose low-production specialty numbers, such as orchard tractors, Hi-Crops, and the like. These variations make the John Deere tractor especially interesting to the collector.

Characteristics of the John Deere Tractor

In 1914, tractors had no conventional layout. Steam traction engines of the time typically had a crankshaft lying transverse to the direction of travel. Thus, it was not surprising that Waterloo chose a similar arrangement for its Waterloo Boy kerosene tractor.

The orientation of the two-cylinder engine in the Waterloo Boy was with the cylinder heads to the back. The engine drove the wheels through the clutch, a simple transmission and differential, and directly into large ring gears mounted inside the rear wheels. Because of the engine's orientation, the engine-wheel gear mesh was at the front of the wheel.

When Deere purchased the firm, Waterloo was already working on an improved tractor with the engine mounted cylinder-head-for-

The innovative knee action Roll-O-Matic front wheel arrangement. The two front axles were connected in such a way that when one wheel was forced up (say, to step over a 4in-high rock), the opposite wheel was forced down an equal amount (4in), but the front of the tractor would rise only half of that (2in). The effect was exactly the same as that experienced with a wide front, thereby making the two versions ride equally well.

A rare 1938 Model BNH, one of only sixty-five built. This one is owned by Bruce Johnson of Lily Lake, Illinois, president of the local chapter of the Two-Cylinder Club.

THE STORY of John Deere Tractor popularity is one of the most unusual in modern times. It goes back to 1924 when the first tractor to bear the John Deere name—the two-cylinder Model "D"—was introduced.

Competition was extremely keen; the trend in tractor engines was toward multi-cylinders.

If ever a newcomer had to make good every step of the way, it was this *two-cylinder* tractor. *And make good it did!* Skepticism gave way to enthusiasm as owners and neighbors watched it perform ... verified its extremely low operating costs ... marveled at its simple, rugged construction.

The "D" became extremely popular. Other John Deere *two-cylinder* models followed until there was a size and type for every farm. Today, these now-familiar green-and-yellow tractors dot the countryside and their owners are numbered in the hundreds of thousands.

This overwhelming, ever-increasing demand for John Deere Tractors is convincing proof of the soundness of *exclusive* John Deere *two-cylinder* design—the design that offers you greater economy, greater dependability, longer life.

Refined in many ways but unchanged in its fundamental advantages, *two-cylinder* design in the new Models "A," "B," and "G" Tractors is your assurance of their *proved* performance.

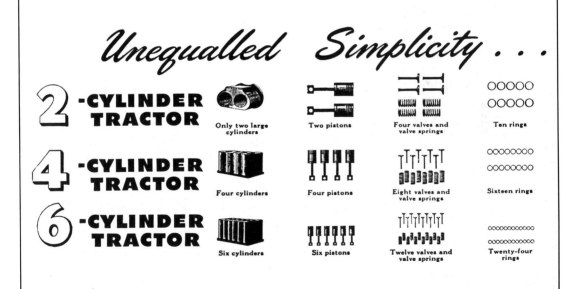

Deere & Co. always promoted the "Unequalled Simplicity" of its two-cylinder engine, as shown in this Deere brochure from 1951. *Deere & Company*

ward. This design used chain drives from the differential shafts to the rear wheels, rather than the large open gear inside the wheels. The chain-drive arrangement gave better weight distribution and more design flexibility and was the basis for the first volume-produced Deere tractor, the Model D. In subsequent tractors, except those with vertical engines, this cylinder-head-forward arrangement was continued. The chain drive was retained on the GP, but most of the rest of the tractors, except for some of the Hi-Crop models, were all-gear drive.

Two basic types of John Deere two-cylinder tractors were produced: the horizontal, cross-engine type and the vertical, inline-engine type. The baby Deere L line and the M and its successors were of the latter type. These used driveshafts between the engine output and the transmission. Their layout was more like that of competing tractors. All these vertical-engine John Deere tractors used a foot-operated clutch, rather than the traditional John Deere hand clutch.

A characteristic of interest in the horizontal-engine Deere tractors was the method of hand starting. Instead of turning a crank, the operator simply rolled the flywheel through a compression stroke, while standing on the ground alongside the tractor. This position allowed the operator to actuate any controls, such as the choke or throttle, without having dual controls. This method was touted as being safer than the hand-cranking method, which it likely was. Nevertheless, electric starting was a welcome addition when it became available in 1939.

It seems the need always exists for a more powerful tractor and for a smaller tractor. Over the years, each John Deere model grew in horsepower until it approached the original level of the next one up. Thus the B grew

This early, styled Model B has the optional fenders and lights.

from 16hp in 1935 to almost 28hp in 1952. To fill the void, the H was introduced in 1939 at 13hp. As the H evolved into the 40 in 1953, horsepower grew to 21.5, and finally, when the 40 became the 430 in 1958, horsepower was at 30.

The small L and LA utility tractors, although highly prized by collectors, were not big sellers when new, averaging a little under 3,000 units a year over its nine-year life span. Nevertheless, these little beauties filled a real niche in the farmer's tractor requirements. They were excellent cultivating and utility machines of about 10hp. The LA even had a standard PTO for such jobs as running shellers and augers.

As time went on, John Deere tractors were industry leaders in innovations. The GP introduced the mechanical power implement lift in 1928. This feature became hydraulic on the new A introduced in 1934, and with it, another industry first: adjustable rear wheel spacing. In 1937, the exclusive knee action Roll-O-Matic ride improvement device was made available on tractors with two-wheel narrow fronts.

Thus, while the John Deere tractor was undergoing continuous change and improvement, its configuration stayed much the same from 1924 through 1960. Besides engine orientation (horizontal or vertical), one other notable line of demarcation divided the tractor family: styling, which hit Deere in 1938.

Enter Henry Dreyfuss

The old saying, Handsome is as handsome does, certainly applied to the farmer's idea of tractor styling in the mid-thirties. To be a farmer in that era, one had to be somewhat pragmatic just to survive. Nevertheless, some tractor manufacturers were attempting to combine form and function as early as 1920—as did the Peoria Tractor Company with its Streamline, for example. By 1935, many tractor makes had styled radiator grilles, which had been the key styling item for the automobile industry since about 1932.

In other industrial areas, pleasing aesthetic proportions were in vogue on products from trucks to telephones, and some well-known designers had achieved a measure of prominence. One of these was Henry Dreyfuss of

A 1937 unstyled Model L, with a nice umbrella. This one is owned by Harold Dobbratz of Woodstock, Illinois.

The flywheel of a late, styled Model G with the cover removed. Note the angled ramps around the hole in the center. In the event of failure of the electric starter, an extension shaft with tangs was inserted into the hole, and the steering wheel was removed and attached to the extension shaft, which placed the steering wheel outside of the rear tire. Then, the steering wheel could be gripped and turned to roll the engine through a compression stroke for manual starting.

15

New York City. The story has it that in the fall of 1937, Deere sent one of its development engineers unannounced to engage Dreyfuss for the task of styling the tractor line. The engineer showed up at Dreyfuss' office in a fur coat and a straw hat, which greatly impressed the designer with what he considered to be the state of cultural awareness in the rural community. This so struck the designer with the potential for redesigning a

You ride in GREATER COMFORT

EXCLUSIVE ROLL-O-MATIC FRONT WHEELS
CUT FRONT-END BOUNCE IN HALF!

ROLL-O-MATIC is an exclusive John Deere Tractor feature that materially reduces operator fatigue and insures a degree of riding comfort unobtainable in a tricycle-type general-purpose tractor equipped with conventional dual front wheels.

You can't help but notice the difference—in the easier, smoother, surer-footed way the tractor steers over rough ground . . . on sidehills . . . in furrows . . . on top of beds . . . along the contour . . . in practically all operating conditions.

Even with manual steering, there's no fighting the wheel, no creeping, no weaving from side to side. Steering is much easier because the load is always equalized *between both front wheels*. Riding is greatly improved because *up-and-down movement of the front end is cut exactly in half as the tractor travels over rough ground*. With just a guiding hand on the wheel, the tractor literally climbs out of furrows . . . "walks" right over obstructions . . . operates in rough fields with greater stability.

Many Advantages

At the left, are two John Deere Tractors. One is equipped with conventional rigid front wheels; the other with Roll-O-Matic. The left front tires of both are resting on a rock 5 inches high. Notice that the entire front end of the conventional tractor has been forced to rise the full 5 inches and that one tire is taking the full load. Now look at the tractor equipped with Roll-O-Matic. Here, the rise is only 2-1/2 inches—*exactly half that of the conventional tractor*—and each tire is taking its full share of the load.

By minimizing the up-and-down movement of the front end and equalizing the load between *both* front wheels, Roll-O-Matic provides a smoother, more comfortable ride, and greatly increases front tire life.

THE CONVENTIONAL WAY....

THE ROLL-O-MATIC WAY....

John Deere's exclusive Roll-O-Matic reduced wheel bounce on the front end and greatly increased operator comfort. It was a revolutionary feature when it made its debut. *Deere & Company*

tractor that he returned that same day to Waterloo with the Deere engineer.

Dreyfuss made the deal with Deere officials, and within a month, he had a wooden mock-up of a new version of the Model B ready for review. The functional beauty of it startled the Waterloo team, and they went for it. This was much more than a radiator grille addition. In many ways the styling was indeed functional. For example, the striking new hood was slimmer, enhancing cultivator visibility, and the new radiator cover, more than just a grille, protected the cooling system from collecting debris.

In an incredibly short time, the Deere-Dreyfuss team brought both the A and B styled models out for the 1939 model year. Their acceptance by the customers led to a styling improvement program that continues to this day. Completion of the initial styling program took eleven years—owing in part to the intervention of World War II—with the venerable AR (Regular) and its orchard running mate, the AO (Orchard), which were the last to receive the treatment, in model year 1949.

The action of Deere's famous Roll-O-Matic front end is shown here. The wheels were geared together so that when one went up over a bump, the other went down a like amount, thus raising the front of the tractor only half as far as it would go with the rigid front.

The 1939 Model AWH on rubber. *Deere & Company*

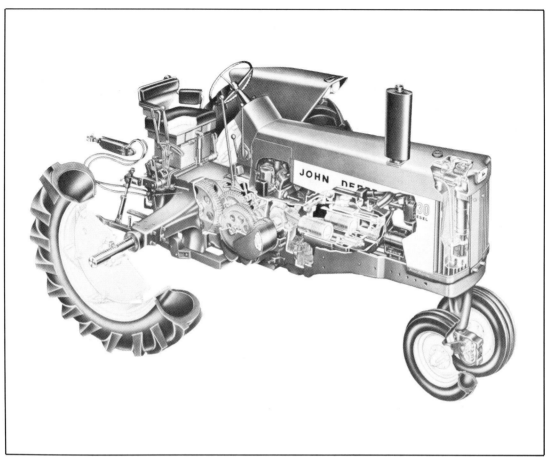

A sectional drawing of the Model 730 shows the layout of Deere's classic two-cylinder general-purpose tractor. *Deere & Company*

Chapter 2

Rating System, John Deere Model and Serial Numbers

Antique tractor collecting is a matter of the heart and consequently does not lend itself to digital quantification. Nevertheless, a certain amount of numerical measurement does help in communication and in determining how much a tractor is worth.

Star Rating System

A star rating system has become a standard among collectors of motor vehicles; however, for each type of vehicle, some special notes are required. Essentially, the star system is based on investment considerations, as follows:

★★★★★ Five stars—the best investment. Tractors with a five-star rating are expensive, but continued appreciation can be expected. These are most often sold or traded between major collectors without the general public or lesser collectors being aware of their availability. Most likely, they are already in first-class condition.

★★★★ Four stars—excellent investment potential. Four-star-rated tractors are still quite expensive, but appreciation is likely to outstrip inflation. These too are most often traded between enthusiasts-collectors.

★★★ Three stars—very good investments, if ownership satisfaction is considered. Inflation will probably about equal the amount of appreciation on a three-star tractor in fairly good condition. Finding one of these in unrestored condition or at an unnaturally low price presents the neophyte collector with the best opportunity to go big time.

★★ Two stars—good investments, but with cost of ownership. Fairly new or high-production (common) models fall in the two-star category. Opportunities could exist among limited edition, or specialized, newer models, for the collector who is in it for the long haul.

★ One star—marginal or poor investments. One-star vehicles were poor invest-

A beautifully restored 1936 Model D, owned by Mike and Jackie Williams of Clinton, Iowa.

A beautifully done 1934 Model A, owned by Jim Quinn of East Peoria, Illinois. Quinn has five other John Deere tractors in his collection. He says he was frustrated as a kid because his family didn't have John Deere tractors. So now he's compensating.

This is one of only 2,019 Model LI tractors made. The LI was technically the same as the L, except for its wider and lower stance.

ments in the first place, with few or no redeeming mechanical or aesthetic qualities. Those completely wrecked or those virtually destroyed by modification also fall into this category, and such would be the only John Deeres that could be one-stars.

The star rating system is used throughout this book, but you should not substitute the system for good judgment. The John Deere collector often cannot define the reason that owning tractors gives a satisfaction that transcends monetary growth. He or she is more akin to the motorcycle enthusiast than to the stamp collector. To this type of collector, the collection is not a static thing, to be looked at only, but like something alive, to be exercised, used, and enjoyed. Many John Deere enthusiasts get almost as much satisfaction from the good-condition but unrestored 520 that they use every day as they do from the perfectly restored and rare Model 80 or the like that they have under plastic in a special garage.

It is not likely that pure investors will be trading antique John Deere futures anytime soon, and today, the typical John Deere collector is generally interested more in physical, mental, and audible satisfactions than in monetary appreciation.

Class Rating System

Another type of rating system is the class system used by antique and collectible car people to define the condition and state of restoration of their vehicles. This system is especially helpful in over-the-phone dealings or in advertisements for collector magazine sales.

Class 1—excellent
Class 1 tractors have been restored to current professional standards in every area or are completely original. All components are operating. In all appearances, these vehicles are brand-new. In other words, class 1 vehicles are in concours condition.

Class 2—fine
Tractors categorized as class 2 include well-done or superior restorations along with excellent well-maintained originals showing minimal wear.

Class 3—very good
The class 3 rating is used for a completely operable original, an older restoration now showing wear, and an amateur restoration that is presentable and serviceable inside and out but not a class 1 or 2. Also in this class are good partial restorations with parts to complete, and other variations on the theme.

Class 4—good
Class 4 tractors are operable or need minor work to become operable. They include deteriorated or poorly accomplished restorations and vehicles in need of complete restoration but mostly usable as they are.

The restoration of this late, unstyled Model A is nearing completion in the shop of Lyle Pals of Leaf River, Illinois

Class 5—restorable

Tractors rated class 5 need complete restoration. They are not drivable but are not weathered, wrecked, or stripped to the point of being useful only for salvage.

Be aware that two definite approaches are used to restore old tractors: restoring to original and refurbishing to serviceable. When considering the class rating, only the former is appropriate. It is a travesty to carelessly refurbish, rather than restore, a unique or rare—4 or 5 star—tractor without attention to correct originality. Plenty of 2 or 3 star tractors can be fixed up (refurbished) as work tractors without messing up a valuable antique.

Model and Serial Numbering Systems

Like model designations at most old-line companies, those at Deere were originally derived through a system understood only by the insiders. Yet, products came to be known by these model numbers or letters, rather than by names, as is often the case with automobiles. Tractors, in recent years, haven't been given names like Firebird or Toronado. Perhaps a marketing opportunity was missed. In the old days of steam, names like Conquerer, Rusher, and Champion were common.

Deere's early practice of assigning letter designations to models was inherited from the Waterloo Boy outfit, which used model and style letter designations. Deere's first proprietary production tractor, the Model D, was actually the fourth of a series of competing style designs undertaken between 1919 and 1922 for a Waterloo Boy replacement: Styles A, B, C, and finally D, which became the Model D.

An early, styled Model AN with a single front wheel. This AN also has a nice set of round-spoke rear wheels.

The use of letters for model designations almost ended with the D. The next tractor developed by Deere was to be the Model C—the third type in a design competition. Its designator was changed to GP for General Purpose, because of the success of the new Farmall, which was billed as a general-purpose tractor.

Things soon got back on the letter-designator track, however, when in the early thirties, in the midst of the Great Depression, the decision was made to introduce two new tractors. Regardless of design competitions, these were to be the Models A and B. From then on, models were more or less alphabetical, with the exceptions of the E, F, I, J, and K.

The letter E was used for stationary engines. The Model G would have been the F but was changed to the G because Farmalls were given F designations such as F-20. The I designation was, of course, used for signifying industrial tractor versions, such as the AI for the Industrial version of the Model A.

The Model R was also an exception. The letter *R* had been used as a subdesignation signifying the conventional, or regular, layout. The Model R was originally intended as a replacement for the Model D, which came only in the regular, or standard-tread, front end. The smaller D stayed in demand for several more years, though, so the R got its own designation.

Each model could have many subvariations. With the exceptions of the D, the R, and the baby Deere L and LA, the basic model designation signifies a general-purpose row-crop tricycle configuration with two front wheels close together. The D and R came only as regulars, with wide front ends and straight front axles. The L-series versions were all wide-front configurations, which meant the kingpin housings extended down from the front axle to provide higher clearance. If all this is confusing, the original GP is not in the general-purpose convention at all, but has a wide front end with an arched axle.

As stated earlier, the basic model designation, such as Model A, indicates the general-purpose version with the two-wheel tricycle configuration. The following list indicates the configuration designator custom that is followed for all models:

AN—single front wheel
AW—adjustable axle, wide front
ANH—high clearance, single front wheel
AWH—high clearance, adjustable axle, wide front
AR—regular (lowboy), or standard-tread, configuration, sometimes called wheatland tractors
AO—orchard configuration
AI—industrial configuration
A–Hi-Crop—extrahigh clearance

Serial Numbers

The attempt was made at Deere to devise a simple and understandable serial numbering system early on. As is often the case with best-laid plans, things went awry. The early Ds conflicted with the last of the Waterloo Boys. The company produced so many versions of the Model C and the subsequent GP, many of which were rebuilt into different variations and renumbered, that it's a wonder track was kept.

Things went from bad to worse as time went on, with gaps in the numbering and widely different numbering for similar tractors (see the "Collecting Comments" sections for each model in subsequent chapters of this book). It was not until the number-designated models—the 50, 60, and so forth—that the system finally worked out with serials beginning with 5 million, 6 million, and so forth. This system was actually begun with the baby Deere Model 62, which used serial number 621000 for the first unit, but Deere soon got off track with the subsequent Models L, LI (Industrial), and LA. One interesting series is that of the M, MT (Tricycle), and MC (Crawler), all of which have individual serial numbering sequences beginning with 10001.

Chapter 3

How to Buy a Collector Tractor

Many old-tractor enthusiasts have eased themselves into tractor collecting while hardly being aware of what they were doing. Some got involved in collecting by not trading in their old tractor when buying a new one for the farm, thinking they'd use it for a backup. After a lifetime of farming, they find themselves with an actual history of a tractor manufacturer stashed behind a barn.

For some others, however, getting involved in collecting tractors, especially John Deere tractors, is a conscious decision, based on an appreciation for fine old machinery and the technology of the times the tractors represent.

There are as many reasons for becoming a John Deere collector as there are readers of this book. Some collectors may have learned to drive on a particular model; some may have struggled with a lesser brand of tractor while envying the John Deere owner in the next field; some may just like green and yellow. Whatever the reason, if you're new at

The Model LI, like the L, weighed in at just over 1,500lb, whereas the LA weighed 2,200lb.

Model LI serial number 501323. Owner Dale Thompson of Genoa, Illinois, is at the wheel at the Sycamore Thresheree in Illinois.

the game, here are some advice and some cautions for the novice.

Perhaps the first decision you should make is whether you are interested in a 100 percent original restoration or if you just want to have a nice old tractor around to help you garden and make firewood.

Be advised that those who desire originality go all the way! Originality means not using modern-tread tires. It means using wiring, hose clamps, spark plugs, and tire valve caps from the tractor's era. It means being a stickler for details most people wouldn't notice. This level of restoration is essential in order to realize the potential value of a rather rare specimen, but if you have just a run-of-the-mill tractor, maybe something less than original will be sufficient.

If you already own the tractor, then neither the decision making nor the buying problem will be necessary. If, however, you have decided which John Deere model you want and the level of restoration you are prepared to handle, but you don't already own the tractor, then the acquisition phase is next on your list.

The handy check list included in the next section of this chapter will help you organize your thoughts in making a buying decision and will also help you arrive at an offer price for the tractor.

When considering the purchase of a tractor located some distance from your base of operations, get as much information on its condition as you can before making the trip. You might consider sending the check list to the owner and asking that it be filled out and returned. Also ask for some photographs to be sent. Even with precautions, don't be surprised if things are not all that you expected.

It is best to have a price in mind when you first contact the prospective seller, but it is up to the seller to quote the asking price first. The same is true of auctions; have your upper-limit dollar figure firmly in mind before the bidding starts. With the individual seller, you usually start at the asking price and bargain downward; with the auction, you do the opposite. If you find that you and the seller are too far apart, tell the seller how

If one is a correctness fanatic, the tread pattern on these rears is not right for the tractor's vintage. Because of the increasing difficulty in obtaining old tires in as good condition as the restored tractor, many collectors are overlooking this problem. Since the late seventies, tire manufacturers have gone to a 35-degree pattern, rather than the 45-degree pattern previously used.

My 1948 Model B in the before condition. It looked as though it had been ridden hard and put away wet, as one old-timer said of it.

you arrived at your figure (based on similar sales, advertisements, or estimated value upon completion), then give the seller your name and phone number on paper and leave. If your facts are convincing, the seller may come around, but you'll not likely cause the seller to change the price a lot, unless she or he has time to check out your logic.

Don't overlook the opportunity for barter in the transaction. Perhaps you have something to trade or can provide some kind of professional service for the seller. Also, look for things to be thrown in on the deal. For example, the seller may be in a position to transport the tractor home for you, or you may require that the seller do some work on it before you take it away.

Once you've struck a deal, you'll be expected to come up with an acceptable form of payment—assuming it wasn't a complete barter deal. If you are close to home, matters are simplified: write a check for the amount, wait for the check to clear, and then pick up your tractor. If waiting is not acceptable, then you'll need cash, a certified check, or traveler's checks.

If you bring a certified check to your initial meeting with the seller, it will not likely be for the right amount. Make it out for your initial offer amount, then at the time of purchase add to it with cash or traveler's checks to bring the amount up to the agreed-upon price. If the amount of the transaction is small or if the difference between the cashier's check and the selling price is not too great, some sellers may accept a personal check, but that had better be established early on.

Tractors are unlike automobiles in that they do not have officially registered titles. How do you know, or how can you find out, if the

My 1948 Model B at Polacek Implement, ready for final paint. David Polacek, standing behind, is the painter. Polacek Implement is a family-run business in Phillips, Wisconsin, where work is done on a variety of old tractors. Having once been an Allis-Chalmers dealer—he is now a Ford–New Holland dealer—Polacek has an especially good stock of Allis parts.

person you are bargaining with really owns the tractor in question? One of the first things you should ask the prospective seller is how long he or she has had the tractor and where it came from. It's a good thing to ask, at that point, if the seller still has the bill of sale. If the seller doesn't and has not had the tractor long, he or she should be willing to go back to the previous owner to get one. If the seller claims to be the original owner of a fifty-year-old tractor and has no purchasing paperwork, you'll have to use your best judgment.

Be sure, when you get your bill of sale, that it includes the correct serial number or other identification. If the dollar amount is very large or if you are uneasy about the legality of the sale, you might require notarization of the bill. At least you will have some recourse if, after you've completed the restoration, you find out you have to give the tractor back.

Once the money has changed hands and you've got the bill of sale, you are the owner. Ordinarily, your homeowners insurance will be sufficient protection for liabilities during restoration, unless you are restoring tractors as a business; then check with your agent. If you transport the tractor home yourself, your regular truck and trailer insurance should apply to cargo. If the value of your purchase is great, you might be wise to talk to your agent about special coverage for it while in transit and while under restoration.

On the way home with your tractor, you may want to get some things done. You may want to take it to a place that has an engine degreasing service and have the whole tractor done. If you are going to tear down the tractor, and assuming you have already done your best to operate it to determine its condition, you may want to stop at a service station and have the oil, fuel, antifreeze, and tire liquid removed. You can, of course, remove these items in your own shop and then take them to a disposal facility, if you choose, but for most of us, this can be a messy procedure.

Two-Cylinder magazine, the organ of the Two-Cylinder Club's worldwide member-

The finished product: the Model B after its paint job. The taller plain muffler is correct for the 1948 B.

The 1948 Model B sports a new set of Firestone tires, even though the tread angle is wrong for a tractor of this period.

ship, has an excellent article called "Collection Protection" in the May–June 1991 issue. It contains some advice by Craig Beek, manager of Corporate Security for Deere, about precautions to take to avoid financial and legal disappointments with collectible tractors. It is reprinted here by permission.

Buyer's Check List

You've been checking "For Sale" ads, farm sale flyers, *Green Magazine*, and *Two-Cylinder* magazine for months trying to get a lead on a John Deere Model M. You have it in your mind; that is the John Deere for you. Finally, in the "Farm Equipment" section of your local paper, you see it:

For Sale—JD-M, 1950, completely gone over, call . . . You quickly call, find out the seller wants $1,500, and get directions. When you get there, you see that indeed the tractor has been "gone over"; it's just been painted with a broom. The tires are bad, the battery is dead, and the radiator is dripping.

Antique tractor buying can be highly charged emotionally. The high expectations of the search may be followed by the dashed hopes of finding a class 5 when you expected a class 3. This, then, is the purpose of the following check list: to take tractor evaluation out of the realm of emotions, as much as possible.

For best results, take this check list with you when you go to evaluate a tractor for purchase. Check the items off as they appear on the list, making notes on each section as you go. The purpose of this is twofold: first, it's an orderly way to complete the evaluation with as much rationality as possible, and second, it gives you a good record of the evaluation for comparison with those of other tractors you find. The check list will be followed by explanations of the items and what to look for.

General Appearance
Sheet metal, grille, and fenders
Tires and wheels
Steering wheel
Exhaust
Oil, water, and fuel system (for leaks)
Model designation
Serial number

Steering
Steering wheel free play
Kingpin free play
Radius rod free play
Front wheel bearing free play
Drag arm or arms free play

Engine
Evidence of crack repair in block and head
Oil in crankcase
Filter in place
Water in crankcase
Water in radiator
Oil in water
Belts
Hoses
Radiator cap
Air cleaner
Carburetor controls
Fuel tank and fuel in tank
Fuel filter, sediment bowl, and shutoff (to see if it is turned on)

Electrical
Battery in place, condition, and water

Ring-type drawbar loops are much sought after by collectors for the older tractors.

Cables and terminals
Generator and brushes
Starter—visible condition
Key and switch—location and operation
Ammeter indication—key on and off
Plug wire condition
General wiring condition
Lights

Clutch and Transmission
Clutch operation
Shift lever operation
Oil level
Water in oil
Leaks, welds, and repairs

Rear Axle
Housing cracks, repairs, and leaks
Lubricant level and water in lubricant
Axle wheel seals
Brakes and linings, and linkage

After Starting:
Engine
Oil pressure
Smoke—tailpipe and breather
Knocking
Missing
Temperature stabilization
Throttle response—revolutions per minute
(rpm) range and governor operation
Oil, water, and hydraulics leaks
Starter operation
Generator charging

Clutch and Transmission
Clutch releasing completely
Gear selection
Clutch engaging smoothly
Clutch slippage
Free pedal
PTO operation

Brakes
Left and right brake power

Hydraulic System
Lift ability
Leak-down
Smoothness

Road-Field Test
Steering shimmy and binding
Brakes
Engine operation under load

Hydraulics operation
Water temperature
Inappropriate noises

Comments to the Buyer's Check List

It is important that the "before starting" tests be done before attempting to start the engine, unless the tractor has been recently run. Not only will this prevent damage from things like lack of oil, but it will allow you to check for water in the oil, or oil in the water, before operation gets everything mixed up. It will, in addition, serve as a setup check, so you don't, for example, attempt to start the engine with the fuel shut off.

The general appearance items are self-explanatory, except for model designation and serial number. These are included so that proper credit will be given if the tractor is historically significant or rare. Lack of definite evidence of model designation or serial number can impede the acquisition of parts and may indicate that the configuration is not original. Generally, the serial number is the only "hard data" on the bill of sale, by which to identify the tractor.

Another important item under this heading is tires. With a new set of current-production tires costing between $600 and $1,000, their condition vitally affects the value of the tractor. To obtain good tires with tread appropriate to the year of the tractor can be difficult or even impossible, and costly. Note that tire manufacturers have changed their marking standards since most of the two-cylinders were built. The first number used to be based on tread width; now it's based on the maximum width of the mounted and inflated tire. Thus, what was an 8-32 is now marked 8.3-32. The specifications listed in chapters 4 to 10 of this book use the original designations.

Steering wheel free play of 2in, measured at the rim, is about the limit of acceptability for more-or-less modern tractors. Obviously, the chain steering of a Waterloo Boy R will be more sloppy, as will the steering of other earlier models lacking provision for wear adjustment.

As you make the engine checks, make the engine ready to start—that is, open the fuel shutoff, add oil and water as necessary, and so forth—if the engine is operable. If the

The owner of this 1950 Model MT refused to consider selling. "I use it to drive my saw rig," he said; "I'd just have to get another one."

engine is inoperable, do your best to determine why. Is compression developing? Is spark occurring? Is the fuel getting through? Is the engine "stuck"? A truly stuck engine can be disaster, but the John Deere two-cylinders can often be "unstuck" by liberally applying penetrating oil, or WD-40, and then slowly towing them in top gear and gingerly engaging the clutch. If the tires slide, let the oil soak for another day or two. Many unstuck two-cylinders operate perfectly after undergoing this procedure.

The ammeter indication item is intended to show that the ignition system and switch are functional, by having you observe an indication of "discharge" when the switch is turned on.

It is important to ascertain that the clutch is actually released when the pedal or lever is in the release position and that the transmission is actually in neutral before you attempt to manually start the engine. Failure to do so could result in your being run over!

After Starting

It's best to check the hydraulics with a heavy implement such as a plow or mower deck. The system should be able to raise and hold anything designed for it with ample reserve. With the engine off, the system should not let the implement down for at least 10 minutes.

Ideally, you can operate the tractor in a field with an implement such as a plow or mower. You should also take it where you can operate it at top road speed. Try all the gears and the brakes. Operate it long enough for things to get warm. Listen for any unusual sounds as it warms up.

Summary

Remember, with all these tests, the main things you are to determine are these: is the price fair, and do you want to get involved in the amount of work required to put the tractor into the shape you desire?

Chapter 4

Waterloo Boy

The First Two-Cylinder

The Waterloo Boy was a direct descendant of the world's first successful internal-combustion traction engine. It was developed by John Froehlich of Froehlich, Iowa, in 1892. Froehlich mounted a single-cylinder Van Duzen engine on Robinson steam tractor running gear. With this tractor, Froehlich completed a fifty-day threshing run, both pulling and powering the thresher, and threshing some 72,000 bushels of small grain.

Later in 1892, Froehlich joined with others to form the Waterloo Gasoline Traction Engine Company, which twenty-six years later was purchased by Deere. Four Froehlich tractors were built, two of which were sold. Neither of the tractors that were sold satisfied its purchaser, and both were returned to Froehlich.

Life in the tractor business was precarious, to say the least. Several new models were developed by Waterloo, but only one of each was ever sold. Meanwhile, the company was having some success selling stationary engines, so in 1895, it reorganized and dropped the word Traction from its name. With this change, Froehlich also left the company.

By 1906, six engine models carrying the trade name Waterloo Boy were in production. Still, tractor experiments continued unabated.

In 1911, A. B. Parkhurst from Moline, Illinois, joined Waterloo, bringing with him

The large Waterloo factory as depicted by an artist in a bucolic setting in the early teens. *Deere & Company*

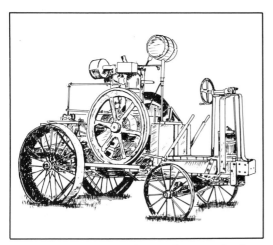

The 1892 Froehlich traction engine was the fore-runner of the Waterloo Boy. It was the first internal-combustion traction engine that could move itself both backwards and forwards. After a successful season of custom threshing with his machine, John Froehlich was instrumental in forming the Waterloo Gasoline Traction Engine Company, which was taken over by Deere in 1918. A replica of this historic tractor now stands in the lobby of Deere World Headquarters in Moline. *Reed Gerber*

three tractors of his own design, with two-cylinder, two-cycle engines. The cylinder arrangement was horizontally opposed. This arrangement was continued on the first Waterloo Boy tractors, the L and LA. The L was a three-wheel, one-wheel-drive model; the LA was the same tractor converted to a four-wheel, two-wheel-drive model.

Only a few of the Models L and LA were sold, as the horizontally opposed engine proved unsatisfactory. A new side-by-side, two-cylinder, four-cycle engine was designed in early 1914. This was installed on an LA chassis, and it was labeled the Model R. This Model R Waterloo Boy, then, became the first of the long line of successful two-cylinder tractors.

The Model R was sold in thirteen styles, A to M, until 1919. Style N, which became the Model N, was introduced in 1917 and produced until 1924. It was replaced by the first mass-produced tractor bearing the John Deere name: the venerable Model D.

Deere took over Waterloo in 1918, after several years of its own tractor experiments.

A portable engine manufactured by Waterloo to be pulled by horses to wherever it was needed in day-to-day farm work. *Deere & Company*

Competition in the farm machinery business was such, at the time, that Deere officials were afraid of waiting for their own designs to be ready. It also appeared that their indigenous designs would be too expensive. Thus, for $2.1 million, Deere bought the assets of Waterloo and entered the market with a proven design selling at a competitive $850.

The Waterloo Boy came in many variations. Convenience changes were incorporated during the production run of a model. Thus, radiators can be found on either side of the R. Some Rs have vertical fuel tanks, some horizontal. Some Ns have chain steering, although most have the automotive type.

In the United Kingdom, Waterloo Boy tractors were sold under the Overtime trade name. They were generally the same, except for a different color scheme.

Models L and LA

Although not considered as traditional Poppin' Johnny two-cylinders because their engine was of a considerably different type, the L and LA were nevertheless progenitors of the line. Only nine of the three-wheeled Ls were sold.

Some twenty LAs were built in 1914. They had one speed forward, and reverse. Steering of the four-wheeled LAs was by worm-sector gear, a type commonly used in automobiles of the time.

The horizontally opposed engine had a 5.5x7in bore and stroke, operating at

Waterloo Boy Specifications		
Years produced:		1914–1924
First serial number:		1026
Last serial number:		31412
Total built:		31,000 (approx.)
Price, new:		$850 (1917)
	Drawbar	**PTO/Belt**
Engine	**Hp**	**Hp**
5.5x7in	12	24
6x7in	12	25
6.5x7in	16	25
General Specifications		
Engine displacement		
5.5x7in		333ci
6x7in		396ci
6.5x7in		465ci
Engine rated rpm		750
Wheels, standard		
Rear		
R		52x10
N		52x12
Front		28x6
Length		
R		142in
N		132in
Width		72in
Height		63in
Weight		6,200lb
Transmission		
Speeds forward		
R		1
N		2
Reverse		1

The Waterloo Boy Model R, owned by Tony Ridgeway of West Unity, Ohio. Ridgeway also has a Model N.

A Waterloo Boy Model N. Note that the drive gear inside the rim of the rear wheel has a larger diameter than the one on the R.

750rpm. It may not be considered a part of the traditional two-cylinder family because it—like the two-cycle diesel in the last John Deere, the Model 435—had an even firing note, quite unlike the sound of the other Waterloo Boy and John Deere tractors.

Model R

Advertised as the original kerosene tractor, the R was much the same as the L, except most examples were equipped with an engine that had a 6.5in bore, rather than a 5.5in bore. A chain windlass steering system that angled the front axle around a pivot was used. The transmission still had only one speed forward. The R was built between 1914 and 1919.

Model N

The Model N, the final variation of the famous Waterloo Boy, can be distinguished from its predecessors by the size of the large drive gear attached to the rear wheels: on the N, it was nearly as large as the wheels; on the earlier tractors, it was much smaller. The N also sported a two-speed transmission and reverted to the worm and sector type of steering.

Collecting Comments

Following is a chart of versions of the Waterloo Boy by model and style. The star system investment rating is shown for each type. Serial numbers for Waterloo Boy tractors are a confusing mess. The serial numbers of stationary engines were intermingled with those of tractors. The serial numbers of the last batch of Waterloo Boys overlapped those of the new Model D, so a block of ninety-two numbers was taken out of the D sequence for the Waterloo Boys. Besides that, older styles and newer styles were built simultaneously. Although the

A Waterloo Boy Model N. *Deere & Company*

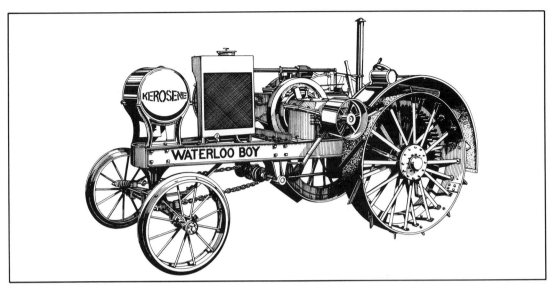

The Waterloo Boy Model N, built from 1917 to 1924. The two-cylinder engine created 12 drawbar hp and 25 belt hp running at 750rpm on kerosene. *Deere & Company*

numbers run consecutively for the year, they are not consecutive for the style. For a complete breakdown of Waterloo Boy serial numbers for each style, see Don Macmillan's book *John Deere Tractors and Equipment: 1837–1959* (see the "Recommended Reading" section near the end of this book).

Serial Numbers and Year Models

The following chart provides a means of determining a tractor's year model by giving the beginning serial number for each production year:

Year	Beginning Serial Number	
	R	N
1915	1026	
1916	1401	
1917	3556	10020
1918	6982	10221
1919	9056	
1920		18924
1921		27026
1922		27812
1923		28119
1924		29520

Rating	Model	Years	Remarks
★★★★★	R, A–D	1914–1915	Integral head and block 5.5x7in engine
★★★★★	R, E–G	1915–1916	Integral head and block 6x7in engine
★★★★	R, H–L	1916–1917	Separate head and block 6x7in engine
★★★★	R, M	1917–1918	6.5x7in engine
★★★★	N	1917–1924	6.5x7in engine
			Two-speed transmission
			Auto Steer after serial number 20834
			riveted frame after serial number 28094
			serial numbers 31320 to 31412 taken out of D sequence

Chapter 5

John Deere Models D, R, 80, 820, and 830

Big Daddy

Considered the ultimate John Deere by the purists, the big daddys were never general-purpose row-crops. These were the Wheatland plowing tractors. They were available only in the standard-tread configuration. They were made to pull!

The term standard-tread signifies a tractor with a beam front axle. This type of tractor has no downward-extending kingpins to raise it above the crop for cultivating. Back in the twenties, when this configuration was established, it was an extension of the running gear used on steam engines and automobiles. As indicated earlier, some of the Waterloo Boy predecessors pivoted this axle

The vast wheat fields of Saskatchewan provide the setting for this styled Model D pulling a Model 36 combine. *Deere & Company*

for steering, as did the steamers, using a chain and windlass system. Thus, in the early days of the tractor business, the straight front axle was considered to be the conventional, or regular, arrangement. And when subsequent general-purpose tractors were introduced with this straight-axle option, they were given the subdesignator R for Regular, such as the BR.

Although some members of the big daddy family were equipped with the hydraulic load-transferring three-point hitch, called the Custom Powr-Trol, they generally relied on weight and a low center of gravity to exert their pull. In addition to pulling, however, they were unexcelled in PTO work, because of their powerful engines.

Another characteristic of this family line is that its versions were not generally equipped with adjustable wheel-tread spacing.

Model D

Beginning in late 1923, the John Deere Model D enjoyed a thirty-year production run—the longest production run of any John Deere; in fact, most likely a longer production run than any other tractor. During this length of time, the D was continually improved yet stayed unmistakably the Model D.

When Deere took over Waterloo in 1918, a replacement for the Waterloo Boy was already in the works. Deere continued this development with a vengeance, testing four styles of tractors through 1922. Seven examples of Style A were produced, including

Model D—The Tractor That Set the Standard for ALL John Deere Tractors

THE spring of 1924 saw the John Deere Model D offered to the farmers of America for the first time. It was an instant success. It sold itself on the basis of its performance in the field, its economy, its simplicity, and its accessibility.

The engineers at the John Deere Tractor Factory had four things in mind when they designed the first Model D. The first was field performance. They wanted to build a three-four plow, heavy-duty tractor capable of handling—successfully—all those jobs which a tractor of this type is called upon to do.

Next came dependability. Such a tractor must be ruggedly built of quality materials to give its owner efficient performance with the very minimum of repair expense, not only when new, but also after years of service.

The third qualification was simplicity. John Deere engineers believed that farmers wanted a simpler tractor, one that was easier to understand . . . a tractor that they could service themselves right on the farm.

Last, but not least, they had in mind economy of operation. They knew that a tractor which burned low-cost fuels successfully would cut operating costs almost in half. These fuels are not only less expensive per gallon but also more powerful—they contain more heat or power units per gallon.

Although the passing years have seen many refinements and improvements made on the Model D, no change has been made in its basic design. So successful was that basic two-cylinder engine design that, today, it is the foundation of the entire line of John Deere Tractors . . . a line of tractors that is setting the pace for economy, simplicity, dependability.

John Deere Model D with Rubber Tires

High or low pressure tires can be supplied for the John Deere Model D in the following sizes:—
Low pressure, 12.75 x 28 rear; 7.50 x 18 front.
High pressure, 42 x 9 single or dual rear; 36 x 5 front.

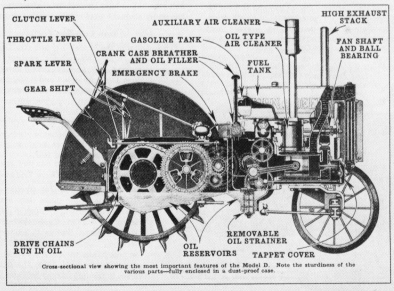

CLUTCH LEVER
THROTTLE LEVER
SPARK LEVER
GEAR SHIFT
CRANK CASE BREATHER AND OIL FILLER
EMERGENCY BRAKE
GASOLINE TANK
AUXILIARY AIR CLEANER
OIL TYPE AIR CLEANER
FUEL TANK
HIGH EXHAUST STACK
FAN SHAFT AND BALL BEARING
DRIVE CHAINS RUN IN OIL
OIL RESERVOIRS
REMOVABLE OIL STRAINER
TAPPET COVER

Cross-sectional view showing the most important features of the Model D. Note the sturdiness of the various parts—fully enclosed in a dust-proof case.

The Model D tractor is featured in the John Deere *Power Farming With Greater Profit* pamphlet produced in 1937. *Deere & Company*

some built prior to the Deere takeover; these were numbered 100 to 106. Seven of Style B were built, numbered 200 to 206. Twelve of Style C were constructed, numbered 300 to 311. And finally, Style D, which became the Model D, was produced.

The second Style D example, number 401, became the first production model. Deere intended to just leave a gap in the Waterloo Boy serial numbering sequence and begin with the D. Therefore, serial number 30401 was assigned to the first production D— Waterloo Boy production not being expected to get that high. Later, when Waterloo Boy production reached serial number 30400, Deere jumped to a block of serial numbers including 31320 to 31412 rather than use the D numbers over. This then caused these ninety-two numbers to be missing from the D sequence in the model year 1924.

The state of the tractor business in the early twenties sheds light on how the D got to be the way it was. The big players were Case, International Harvester (McCormick-Deer-ing), Allis-Chalmers, Fordson, and the General Motors Samson. The tractor was rapidly maturing—taking on its own identity and moving away from being a steam engine with internal combustion.

One prominent feature of the new field was the all-enclosed frameless structure. This was pioneered by the Wallis outfit—by this time part of Case—but had been taken to the ultimate extent on the Fordson. Thus, open drives, such as that of the Waterloo Boy, were rapidly becoming outmoded. One of the prototypes of the D featured an enclosed frame and was known as the bathtub tractor.

A number of designs, including late Waterloo Boy Model Ns, were using double roller chains for final drives. These were easy to enclose and solved a lot of gear deflection problems in the high-torque end of the driveline.

Competition among the giants for the limited amount of business drove prices down. The Fordson sold for a record low of $395 in 1922. Those who could, cut their

The Model D, constructed from 1924 to 1953, was the first Waterloo tractor to bear the John Deere nameplate. *Deere & Company*

prices proportionally; those who couldn't, either relied on exporting or halted production. A great many farmers got a taste of power farming as a result of the tractor price war, but the trend was away from the behemoths and toward lighter-weight equipment. The Fordson weighed less than half what the Waterloo Boy weighed yet had a drawbar pull of more than 75 percent of the Waterloo Boy's.

Accordingly, as the D took shape in 1922 and 1923, it was affected by these technical and market forces. The engine configuration was to be maintained, as that had proved to be one of the best features of the Waterloo Boy. The bathtub-type enclosure was to be adopted. The final drive was to be roller chain. And the tractor was to be lighter, though more powerful; the initial Ds weighed in at about 4,250lb.

One peculiarity of the D was that it began life with a two-speed transmission, whereas even the Fordson had a three speed. It received a third gear in 1935, when all other tractors were going to four. Neither this nor any of the perceived or real shortcomings seem to have hurt the D's popularity, with sales continuing high enough to keep it in the line-up for five years after its replacement, the Model R, came into being.

During its lifetime, the D had two power increases. In 1927, the bore was increased 0.25in; in 1930, the rpm were increased by 100 to 900. Brake horsepower went from 30.4 to 37 to 42. Bear in mind that these are Nebraska numbers, which are not corrected to sea level standard-day conditions. Data indicates the maximum corrected horsepower to be 44.83.

The D was the third John Deere to receive the Dreyfuss styling treatment, although not

The vertical exhaust on the Model D indicates it is a 1931 or later model.

An early Model D spoker. The first 50 built used a 26in spoked flywheel and had the steering wheel on the left side. In 1925, some were made with 24in spoked flywheels and a steering wheel that was centered by means of a universal joint in the shaft. By late 1925, the flywheel was changed to a solid casting, and it remained so throughout the rest of the thirty-year production run. Any Model D with a spoked flywheel is a valuable collector item.

as extensively as the A and B. Nevertheless, the styled D is a handsome tractor.

Collecting Comments

The Model D went into production in early 1923 and the last one was shipped in March of

This early Model D has a brass magneto and, not shown, a brass carburetor. Such items are of utmost importance to collectors.

A derelict styled Model D with a makeshift grille stands moldering in the snow while awaiting some-one's resurrecting touch. Note the big rice tires on the back.

1954, although it was a 1953 model. As the following chart shows, variations were produced in very low numbers, making them more valuable to collectors. Also shown is the star system investment rating for each type.

During the first two years of production, Ds were equipped with a 24in or 26in cast spoked flywheel. These are known today as spokers.

Because of customer demand, the last ninety-two Ds were assembled from spare parts after the production line was broken down. These tractors were built outside in a roadway between two buildings. The workers nicknamed them streeters. Streeters are identified by serial number and are very much sought after by collectors.

Serial Numbers and Year Models

The following chart provides a means of determining a tractor's year model. Model Ds built in 1923 were considered 1924 models.

Year	Beginning Serial Number
1924	30401
1925	31280
1026	35309
1927	43410
1928	54554

Year	Beginning Serial Number
1929	71561
1930	95367
1931	109944
1932	115477
1933	115665
1934	116273
1935	119100
1936	125430
1937	130700
1938	138413
1939	143800
1940	146566
1941	149500
1942	152840
1943	155005
1944	155426
1945	159888
1946	162598
1947	167250
1948	174879
1949	183516
1950	188420
1951	189701
1952	191180
1953	191439

Model D Specifications

Years produced:	1923–1953
First serial number:	30401
Last serial number:	191670
Total built:	160,000 (approx.)
Price, new:	$1,000 (1924); $2,400 (1953)

Engine	Drawbar Hp	PTO/Belt Hp
6.5x7in	22.5	30.4
6.75x7in		
800rpm	28.5	37
900rpm	30.7	41.6
Rubber	38	42.1

General Specifications

Engine displacement			
To serial number 53387			465ci
From serial number 53388			501ci
Engine rated rpm			
To serial number 109993			800
From serial number 109994			900
Wheels and tires, standard			
	Wheels		Tires
Rear	46x12		13.5x28
Front	28x5		7.5x18
	1923–30	1931–34	1935–53
Length	109in	117in	130in
Height to radiator	56in	56in	61in
Weight	4,000lb	5,110lb	5,270lb
Transmission			
Speeds forward			
Early			2
After serial number 119945			3
Reverse			1

Rating	Years	Serial Numbers	Remarks
★★★★★	1923–1924	30401–30450	26in spoked flywheel, welded front axle, left-hand steering, ladder side radiator, 6.5x7in engine
★★★★★	1924	30451–31279	26in spoked flywheel, ladder side radiator, cast front axle
★★★★★	1924–1926	31280–36248	24in spoked flywheel, serial numbers 31320 to 31412 assigned to the Waterloo Boy, not the D
★★★	1926–1927	36249–53387	Solid flywheel, keyed to shaft
★★	1927–1930	53388–109943	Solid flywheel, splined to shaft, 6.75x7in engine
★★★	1931–1934	109944–119099	Right-hand steering, intake and exhaust stacks above hood, 900rpm
★★★	1935–1938	119945–143799	Three-speed
★★	1939–1953	143800–191578	Styled
★★★★	1953	191579–191670	Streeters
★★★★★	1927–1940	53388–150118*	Industrial, serial numbers interspersed

*Randomly intermingled with regular Model D production.

The Model R met Deere's goal of a tractor that combined increased power with a diesel engine. It was constructed from 1949 to 1954. In 1949, it was rated at 34.27 drawbar hp and 43.32 belt hp, according to the State of Nebraska Test. *Deere & Company*

Model R

The Mighty R has probably the most beautiful and best "form-fitting-function" tractor design anywhere, by anybody. Strong statements? Yes, but the R is a strong tractor. It was born of the twin requirements for a growth version of the D for the expanding wheat and rice operations and diesel power in larger tractors for fuel economy.

The R was Deere's first diesel. Fuel cost was a significant consideration in tractor selection, and Deere had gained a reputation for its use of low-cost kerosene-powered equipment. By the early thirties, however, this advantage was beginning to erode as the smaller-displacement, high-compression, high-speed gasoline engine came to maturity. Also, the demand for gasoline, which is made from the same petroleum components as kerosene, was driving the price of ker-

Wheatland farmers were asking for more power in a standard-tread tractor than the venerable Model D could supply, so in 1949 Deere came out with the classic Model R. This was Deere's first diesel engine tractor. It used a gasoline pony motor for starting.

osene upward. Chief Engineer Barrett Rich of Deere concluded, and rightly so, that the phenomenal efficiency of the diesel cycle was the wave of the future.

Diesels are fuel efficient for two primary reasons. First is their compression ratio of over 16:1. Although diesel fuel and kerosene are similar—both have the same British thermal units (Btus) per pound—a spark-ignition kerosene tractor is relegated to a compression ratio of about 4:1. This means that a diesel cylinder with an equivalent displacement will have an expansion ratio four times higher than that of a kerosene cylinder during the power stroke.

The second reason diesels are more fuel efficient is in their lean-mixture ratio. All spark-ignition engines operate on a rich mixture of about twenty parts air for every part fuel. This is fairly constant over the speed range. Diesels, on the other hand, do not have throttle butterfly valves on the air intake. Instead, the engine gets the same gulp of air for each revolution, regardless of speed or load. Engine speed and power are controlled by how much fuel is squirted in by the injectors at the top of the compression stroke. Thus, the diesel always runs on the lean side, especially at idle or low load. Even at full load, the mixture ratio for a diesel is much leaner than that for a gasoline or kerosene engine.

These conditions providing efficiency for diesels also caused hard starting, especially in cold weather. An engine with a 16:1 compression ratio will be much harder to crank than one with a 4:1 ratio. But the 16:1 compression generates compression temperatures of around 1,000 degrees Fahrenheit, which is supposed to cause the fuel to auto ignite. When the engine is cold, it must be cranked with enough vigor that this temperature is attained and is maintained long enough to warm up the vast quantities of cast iron so that combustion isn't quenched.

The first diesel tractor, the Caterpillar Diesel 65, was introduced in 1931. To start the diesel engine, Caterpillar pioneered the use of a small gasoline starting motor called a pony motor. Once the pony was started, the

The left side of the Model R.

cranking time of the diesel was limited only by the pony fuel supply.

Other crawler tractors followed with diesels. In 1932 came the McCormick-Deering T40 diesel, which could be started on gasoline and then switched over to diesel by mechanical devices that shut off part of the combustion chamber to raise the compres-

Model R Specifications		
Years produced:		1949–1954
First serial number:		1000
Last serial number:		22293
Total built:		21,000 (approx.)
Price, new:		$3,650 (1954)
	Drawbar	PTO/Belt
Engine	Hp	Hp
Diesel	45.7	51
General Specifications		
Engine displacement		416ci
Engine bore and stroke		5.75x8in
Engine rated rpm		1000
Tires, standard		
Rear		
Standard		14-34
Optional		18-26
Front		7.5x18
Length		147in
Height		78in
Weight		7,400lb
Transmission		
Speeds forward		5
Reverse		1

A piston, valve, and pushrod from the 18.8ci V-4 pony motor used for a starter in the John Deere diesels. The pony was rated at 5500rpm.

sion. In 1935, this same engine was put in the International Harvester WD-40, the world's first diesel wheel tractor.

It is not surprising, then, that Chief Engineer Rich began looking into a diesel for Deere in 1935. The work began with power units rather than a tractor, because basic experience had to be gained. Several types of starting systems were tried, along with test engines, including the types used by Caterpillar and International Harvester. The pony motor approach was finally selected because of its inherent reliability and because the exhaust from the pony could be routed through diesel engine areas to help warm them up.

By 1940, diesel engine development at Deere had reached a point where it could be incorporated into a tractor, so a design was undertaken that resulted in a tractor not unlike the subsequent Model R, called the MX.

Eight experimental MX tractors were completed in 1941. These were thoroughly tested and then completely redesigned to eliminate weaknesses. The new MX was ready in 1944; five were built. After several more years of rigorous testing, the complete design was again reviewed and a third lot, with eight tractors, was completed in 1947. This final MX

version was very close to the configuration of the production R.

When the new diesel R was introduced in 1949, Deere marketing people were not sure that customers would accept it as a replacement for the D. Advertising of the day pointed out the similarities: the horizontal two-cylinder engine, the frameless structure, the inherent strength and simplicity. It also pointed out the R's advantages: diesel economy, all-gear final drive, and a five-speed gearbox. By adopting the 24.6ci, horizontally opposed, electrically started gasoline pony motor as the starter for the R, Deere allayed many of the farmers' fears about owning a diesel. And it didn't hurt that many returning World War II servicemen were singing the praises of the rugged Caterpillar diesel equipment they had encountered in Alaska, Europe, and the South Pacific.

Model R deliveries began in early 1949. This replacement for the D had 21 percent more power and weighed almost half again as much as the D. The R could handle five 14in bottoms with ease, and the live Powr-Trol, live PTO, soft bench seat, individual brakes, and comfortable steering wheel position meant work was a pleasure. The R could plow a forty in a twelve-hour day and do it on less than 25 gallons of diesel fuel. By contrast, a D would take two days and require almost twice as much fuel.

Collecting Comments

The Model R is an interesting and rewarding tractor to own, but one must remember that a good number of its fascinating qualities come from its massiveness, and therein lies its drawback. A four-ton tractor will likely require a gooseneck trailer, and at least a three-quarter-ton pickup for hauling. And a brand-new set of tires for an R can sometimes double the tractor's price. With that said, however, no finer parade tractor than the R is

Rating	Years	Serial Numbers	Remarks
★★★	1949–1954	1000–22293	Deere's first diesel, 5.75x8in engine, 2.6x2.3in gas pony, 4000rpm

to be found. With the shiny dark green paint, the huge rear tires, and the monstrous engine loafing along at the idle speed of lesser machines, it's the hit of any parade.

The R was built in only one version, so collectibility varies little between examples. As with other John Deere two-cylinders, add a star to the rating for the first and last ten serial numbers and another star for the first and last two serial numbers—unless the model is already a five-star. Add a star to any R equipped with an original factory steel cab as well.

Serial Numbers and Year Models

The following chart provides a means of determining a tractor's year model by giving the beginning serial number for each production year:

Year	Beginning Serial Number
1949	1000
1950	3541
1951	6368
1952	9293
1953	15720
1954	19485

Model 80

Six years after its introduction, the R was replaced by the 80. The year was 1955; the other new number series tractors had made their debut almost three years earlier. The popularity of the R accounts at least partly for the delay. Deere was reluctant to fix something that wasn't broken. Nevertheless, the competitive pressures of the mid-fifties required some updating, so the 80 was born to

The Model 80 arrived in 1955 as a replacement for the famous Model R, still using a diesel engine. It was constructed through 1956. In 1955, it was rated at 46.32 drawbar hp and 57.49 belt hp, according to the State of Nebraska Test. *Deere & Company*

The Model R and the Model 80 generally had the four-spoke steering wheel, unless, on the 80, factory power steering was installed. The later 820 and 830 models had only three spokes, as power steering was standard by then. Somehow, the four-spokes seem more appropriate for these gutsy-looking tractors. The one shown is on an 80.

Model 80 Specifications

	Drawbar	PTO/Belt
Years produced:		1955–1956
First serial number:		8000001
Last serial number:		8003500
Total built:		3,500 (approx.)
Price, new:		$4,200 (1956)
Engine	**Hp**	**Hp**
Diesel	61.8	67.6
General Specifications		
Engine displacement		472ci
Engine bore and stroke		6.125x8in
Engine rated rpm		1125
Tires, standard		
Rear		
Standard		15-34
Optional		18-26
Front		7.5x18
Length		143in
Height		81in
Weight		7,850lb
Transmission		
Speeds forward		6
Reverse		1

bring the model designation in line with the rest.

From all appearances, the 80 was a dead ringer for the R—the epitome of Dreyfuss styling. About the only way you could tell them apart from any distance was that the R had a round flywheel cover, whereas the 80—and subsequent big daddy tractors—had teardrop-shaped covers. Also, the R had a hood medallion, whereas the 80 had the words John Deere above the grille. Internal improvements included the following:

Horsepower was increased by 33 percent through an increase in the bore size to 6.125in from 5.75in and through a raise in the operating speed to 1125rpm from 1000rpm. A new crankshaft with three main bearings was incorporated. As was the R, the 80 was available only with diesel power.

A new 18.8ci displacement V-4 pony starter motor was adopted from the 70 Diesel, which was introduced in 1953. The operating speed of the new pony was 5500rpm, up from the 4000rpm of the two-cylinder unit used on the R.

A six-speed transmission, rather than the five-speed of the R, was used. Power steering was available as an option. This was a welcome addition for a tractor of this size.

Improved optional dual hydraulics was available and an improved optional PTO was offered. A 32.5 gallon fuel tank replaced the 22 gallon unit of the R. Also incorporated was an electric fuel gauge.

A two-position wheel-tread spacing was incorporated—a first for standard-tread trac-

Rating	Years	Serial Numbers	Remarks
★★★★	1955–1956	8000001–8003500	6.125x8in diesel engine, 2x1.5in gas V-4 pony, 5500rpm

Seventy-two-year-old Don Miller of Polo, Illinois, sits atop his pride and joy, a 1955 Model 80. This is the 708th 80 built. Although the 80 is a standard-tread tractor, the tread can be changed to wider-than-standard by reversing the rims.

tors. This was accomplished by providing reversible wheels.

Collecting Comments

Although the 80 made its debut years after the other two-number tractors, its demise came with theirs at the advent of the three-number series. This gave the 80 a production run of only twelve months, plus a week or so. Thus, only about 3,500 were delivered. Only the Model 435 and the GP-P (Potato) had comparable production lives. This makes the 80 a somewhat uncommon but modern tractor, and a great buy for the serious collector.

Add a star to the rating for the first and last ten serial numbers.

Serial Numbers and Year Models

The following chart provides a means of determining a tractor's year model by giving the beginning serial number for each production year:

Year	Beginning Serial Number
1955	8000001
1956	8000755

Model 820

The R and the 80 only whetted the wheat and rice growers' appetite for the big standard-tread tractors. After a little over twelve months of production, the 80 was supplanted by the 820, which looked much the same except for yellow hood side panels.

Other tractors in the new 20 Series had received power boosts, but not the 820. Customers complained that the new 720 Diesel, with its power boost, had closed the gap between the two. The engineers at Deere were fairly well convinced by now that most farmers would absorb all the horsepower made available to them—a belief that would lead to the demise of the two-cylinder in 1960.

The Model 820 Diesel continued the heritage of the Model R Diesel. It was introduced with the 20 Series in 1956 and continued to be offered until 1958. It was rated at 52.25 drawbar hp and 64.26 belt hp, according to the State of Nebraska Test. *Deere & Company*

Therefore, near the middle of its production run, the 820 was given a 12 percent horsepower boost without changing the displacement or operating speed of the engine, by improving the engine's breathing capacity, modifying the pistons for more compression, and improving the injectors.

The big news for the 820, as for the others in the series, was Custom Powr-Trol. This was an improved version of the dual live hydraulic system begun on the R and further improved on the 80. The Custom version incorporated Draft Control, a feature whereby implement loads transmitted forward through the top link—sometimes called the free-link—actually controlled the implement working depth by pushing on the hydraulic control valve.

Draft Control was invented in the thirties by Irishman Harry Ferguson and incorpo-

The flywheel side of a Model 820 with special rice tires and wheels. *Deere & Company*

Rating ★★★	Years 1956–1958	Serial Numbers 8200000–8207078	Remarks 6.125x8in diesel engine, 2x1.5in gas V-4 pony, 5500rpm

rated into the Ford-Ferguson tractor after the famous Handshake Agreement between Henry Ford and Ferguson in 1938. With the dissolution of the Ford-Ferguson agreement in 1947 and with the settlement of the subsequent lawsuit in 1952, the patents for Draft Control were up for grabs, and all the tractor manufacturers rushed to develop their own version. The function of Draft Control was to sense the increasing drag, or draft, of an implement such as a plow owing to changing soil conditions or the like, and to lift by means of the hydraulic three-point hitch the implement until the original draft load was restored. Conversely, the implement would also be lowered to the preset maximum depth in an effort to keep the draft load constant.

In operation, Ferguson's system reacted to increased draft load, say as a plow encountered hard pan, by slightly raising the plow. Not only did this ease the load on the plow, but the act of raising the plow greatly increased the download on the back wheels, which aided traction. As the hard spot was passed and the draft load diminished, the system returned the plow to its preset depth. The Custom Powr-Trol could also independently control two remote hydraulic cylinders on trailing implements.

Other features of the new 820 were power steering as standard equipment, an optional creeper first gear, and the optional Float-Ride seat that could be adjusted to the operator's weight.

Collecting Comments

The 820 was a continuation of the big daddy tradition begun with the Model D and continued with the diesel Rs and 80s. As a collector tractor, it suffers a little in that it wasn't the ultimate Deere that the 830 was. Nor was it as rare as the 80, nor was it the first diesel, as the R was. Nevertheless, since not many of the big Wheatlands of any series

Model 820 Specifications

Years produced:		1956–1958
First serial number:		8200000
Last serial number:		8207078
Total built:		7,000 (approx.)
Price, new:		$4,900 (1958)

Engine Diesel	Drawbar Hp	PTO/Belt Hp
Early	61.8	67.6
After serial number 8203100	69.7	75.6

General Specifications

Engine displacement	472ci
Engine bore and stroke	6.125x8in
Engine rated rpm	1125
Tires, standard	
Rear	
Standard	15-34
Optional	18-26
Front	7.5x18
Length	143in
Height	81in
Weight	8,150lb (with optional Powr-Trol)
Transmission	
Speeds forward	6
Reverse	1

exist, they are all fairly collectible and should be good investments.

Add a star to the rating for the first and last ten serial numbers.

Serial Numbers and Year Models

The following chart provides a means of determining a tractor's year model by giving the beginning serial number for each production year:

Year	Beginning Serial Number
1956	8200000
1957	8200565
1958	8203850

Model 830

Mister Mighty is what advertising copy called the Model 830. It was the ultimate big

The Model 830 made its debut with the 30 Series as a replacement for the 20 Series, with an emphasis on more power and operator convenience and comfort. Introduced in 1958, it continued in production into 1961. It was advertised at 69.66 drawbar hp and 75.6 belt hp. *Deere & Company*

A view from the office of the gigantic Model 830, the ultimate two-cylinder.

daddy tractor, the last of the long green line. The 830 had the same power as the late 820s, but it was upgraded in ways of comfort, convenience, and productivity. Besides ergonomic improvements in seat, controls, and instruments, Mister Mighty was equipped with a standard foot pedal accelerator in addition to the usual hand lever accelerator. Operators had often asked for this convenience item for maneuvering the big tractor with loads such as disks and harrows. Also new for the 830, as for all the 30 Series models, was the big oval muffler. The slow-turning two-cylinder John Deeres were always much easier on the ears than the competition, but the new muffler made them even quieter.

Another new feature with the 830 was the availability of an electric start option instead of the V-4 pony starter. This was a 24 volt system with plenty of power to get the job done in the cold. To further help the 830 in the cold, additional heating elements were installed in strategic spots in the engine.

The big 830 could handle six 14in bottoms or a 20ft disk. Often, multiple loads were applied, such as disks followed by harrows. The 830 was also unexcelled for PTO work. Because of these capabilities, many 830s are

Model 830 Specifications

	Drawbar Hp	PTO/Belt Hp
Years produced:		1958–1960
First serial number:		8300000
Last serial number:		8306892
Total built:		6,893 (approx.)
Price, new:		$5,000 (1960)
Engine		
Diesel	69.7	75.6
General Specifications		
Engine displacement		472ci
Engine bore and stroke		6.125x8in
Engine rated rpm		1125
Tires, standard		
Rear		
Standard		15-34
Optional		18-26
Front		7.5x18
Length		143in
Height		81in
Weight		8,150lb (with optional Powr-Trol)
Transmission		
Speeds forward		6
Reverse		1

At over four tons, the 830 is the giant of the John Deere two-cylinder tractors. This one is equipped with the optional V-4 gasoline starting motor.

A Model 830 in full snort, driving a dynamometer at the Franklin Grove Thresheree in Illinois. This one is making both the owner and the dynamometer operator smile.

still at work and are not ready to be fixed up for the parade circuit.

Collecting Comments

The 830s were the ultimate two-cylinder. They were big. They were impressive. They were heavy. They were expensive to operate in the first place, and they still are: a pair of current 16.2-34 rear tires and tubes cost between $800 and $900 in 1992. And these tires are not something you can mount yourself, unless you have some pretty fancy equipment.

Nevertheless, because they were the last of the line and the top of the line, and because they represent the epitome of the type, the 830s are desirable to collectors. They rate only three stars today, because they are of recent vintage, but add a star for the first ten and last twenty serial numbers, and add another star for the last ten.

Serial Numbers and Year Models

The following chart provides a means of determining a tractor's year model by giving the beginning serial number for each production year:

Year	Beginning Serial Number
1958	8300000
1959	8300727
1960	8305301

Evidence indicates that one 830, serial number 8306892, was built in model year 1961.

Rating	Years	Serial Numbers	Remarks
★★★	1958–1960	8300000–8306892	6.125x8in diesel engine, 24 volt electric start or 2x1.5in gas V-4 pony, 5500rpm

Chapter 6

John Deere Models A, 60, 620, and 630

Big Mama

The big mama line of John Deere tractors began with the Model A in early 1934. Also in the line-up at the time were the Models D and GP. The A, a two-plow tractor, fit nicely between the three-plow D and the one-plow GP. The big difference was that the new A was a true general-purpose row-crop ma-chine. It was designed to counter the Farm-all's pillage of the marketplace.

The Farmall was first announced in 1922 but was not produced in significant numbers until 1926. By the early thirties, it was having the same effect on Deere's market share as the Fordson price war had had in the late

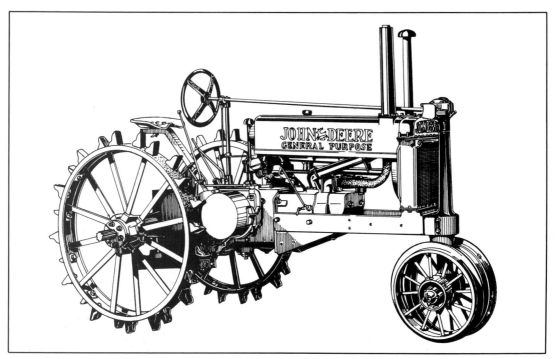

The Model A was constructed from 1934 to 1952. The original 1934 Model A was rated at 16.22 drawbar hp and 23.52 belt hp, according to the State of Nebraska Test. *Deere & Company*

John Deere Model A General Purpose

W HEN the John Deere Model A General Purpose Tractor with adjustable tread was introduced to farmers in the spring and summer of 1934, it met with immediate and widespread acceptance.

In the hands of users, the Model A quickly proved every claim made for it. It met the most exacting needs of farmers in all sections. It established itself as the number one all-around farm tractor value.

During the big swing to tractors in 1935 and 1936, its outstanding design, its ability to do *more work* and *better work* at lower costs, created a demand that taxed the capacity of the big John Deere tractor factory.

Outstanding in Design

The first thing you notice when you look at the Model A is its narrow radiator and fuel tank. No other tractor provides such a perfect view of the work on both sides of the tractor.

The tractor seat is spring-mounted and can be adjusted to the weight of the operator. It places you in a commanding position—well up above the dust. When you take the wheel, you are amazed at the new ease of steering—your automobile steers no easier. You find all the other features you want in *your* tractor—the adjustable rear wheels, the convenient foot brakes that individually control the rear wheels for short turns, the new, hydraulic power lift with cushioned drop, the hand-controlled clutch, the wide, roomy operator's platform, the four forward speeds, the straight line of draft in plowing and the two-cylinder engine design that makes it possible to burn low-cost fuels *successfully.*

Outstanding in Performance

The Model A is designed to handle a six-horse load on drawbar jobs, will operate a 22- to 24-inch thresher. With its modern 2- and 4-row equipment, it puts into the hands of one man the working capacity of three to six men using less modern equipment.

It is the ideal tractor for planting and cultivating your row crops. It is ready to prepare seed beds, handle your haying operations, operate your harvesting equipment, cut ensilage, grind feed—to handle any farm job within its power range.

Rubber Tires

The Model A can be furnished with special rear wheels and 9.00 x 36″ low-pressure rubber tires and tubes; special front wheels with 5.25x16″ or 5.50x16″ low pressure rubber tires and tubes.

Skeleton Wheels

The Model A at the right is equipped with skeleton-type rear wheels. This type of wheel is popular in many sections, particularly in sections where the soil is firm or hard.

The unstyled Model A general-purpose tractor as featured in the John Deere *Power Farming With* *Greater Profit* pamphlet produced in 1937. *Deere & Company*

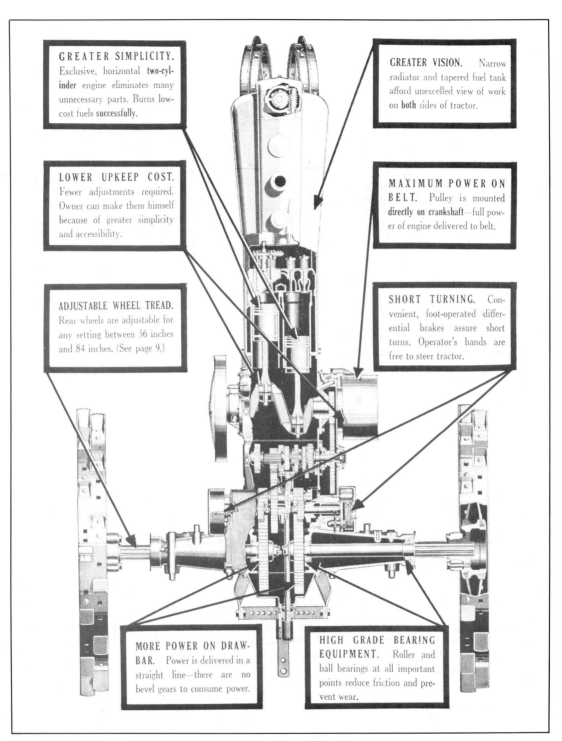

GREATER SIMPLICITY. Exclusive, horizontal **two-cylinder** engine eliminates many unnecessary parts. Burns low-cost fuels **successfully.**

GREATER VISION. Narrow radiator and tapered fuel tank afford unexcelled view of work on **both** sides of tractor.

LOWER UPKEEP COST. Fewer adjustments required. Owner can make them himself because of greater simplicity and accessibility.

MAXIMUM POWER ON BELT. Pulley is mounted **directly on crankshaft**—full power of engine delivered to belt.

ADJUSTABLE WHEEL TREAD. Rear wheels are adjustable for any setting between 56 inches and 84 inches. (See page 9.)

SHORT TURNING. Convenient, foot-operated differential brakes assure short turns. Operator's hands are free to steer tractor.

MORE POWER ON DRAW-BAR. Power is delivered in a straight line—there are no bevel gears to consume power.

HIGH GRADE BEARING EQUIPMENT. Roller and ball bearings at all important points reduce friction and prevent wear.

The benefits of the John Deere two-cylinder tractor advances as shown in a 1941 brochure. *Deere & Company*

twenties. By 1931, the Farmall factory in Rock Island, Illinois, was producing tractors at a rate three times higher than that of Deere's Waterloo works.

Deere's counterattack, in the form of the Model A—and, almost simultaneously, the Model B to replace the GP—was an all-out effort on the part of management to stay in business. One must remember that the early thirties were dire times for world agriculture; in fact, they were dire times for the world's economy. Deere management bet the company on the new tractors, and the bet paid off handsomely. By the end of 1936, despite the hard times, tractor output had doubled, and through 1960, the big mama–size tractors were always either first or second in sales.

During this life span, drawbar horsepower grew from 19 in 1934 to 44 in 1960. The growth clearly relates the revolution that occurred in power farming during that time. As implements and traction improved, more power meant more work per hour. Note that while power and maximum pull more than doubled, the weight went up only 25 percent. Fuel consumption on a horsepower-hour per gallon basis improved almost 60 percent.

A 1934 Model A with an open fan shaft. The first 4,800 or so Model As built had the rotating fan drive shaft partially exposed. After serial number 414808, this shaft, seen above and to the left of the air intake pipe, was fully enclosed.

Thus, a 630 doing twice the work would use very little more fuel than the original A.

Model A

Next to the B, the most popular tractor in Deere's history was the innovative Model A.

This unstyled Model A has a nice set of round-top fenders, which are much sought after by collectors. Note that unstyled Model As and Bs had side-by-side intake and exhaust pipes, as did the Model G. The styled G retained the side-by-side arrangement, whereas the A and B did not.

This 1934 Model A with open fan shaft is in pretty bad shape. This is the way Tom Detweiler found it. Detweiler is a John Deere collector and dealer in antique tractor parts in Spencer, Wisconsin.

55

Does this mean the As are not collectible? Not at all! The A has become the quintessential John Deere for many collectors. Of the many variations produced over the model's nineteen-year run, some were built in limited numbers, which is a prominent collectibility consideration.

Model A production ran from 1934 to 1952. Around 300,000 were built, with many specialized submodels in the series. The A was historic in that it was the first tractor with a hydraulic implement lift, which replaced the mechanical device of the GP. Also featured was the industry's first adjustable-wheel-tread rear axles—a must for true row-crop farming.

Another unique feature of the Model A was its one-piece transmission housing. Previously, castings such as this were made in halves. The new one-piece type allowed more crop clearance and, more important, allowed the drawbar and the PTO shaft to be on the tractor's centerline.

The individual left and right foot brakes, a first on John Deere tractors, were introduced on the Model A.

The Model A was born of the frustration of the Great Depression and of disappointment at the performance of the GP. Deere had several experimental endeavors severely curtailed by the Depression in 1930, including its research farms in the Moline area, but nevertheless, tractor development was aggressively continued.

Farmers had shown their willingness to support a general-purpose tractor, in addition to a plowing–prime mover tractor such as the D. And more power was needed than the GP and Farmall were delivering. Therefore—despite the hard times and shortages of money, both in the company and on the farms—Charles Wiman, head of Deere, put the company on the line for two new models:

A view looking aft from the flywheel side of an early, styled Model A. The lever and the box from which it emanates are for a Behlen Road Gear. Owner Lyle Pals says it operates only if the regular transmission is in neutral; then it will do about 25mph.

Model A Row-Crop Specifications

Years produced:		1934–1952
First serial number:		410008
Last serial number:		703383
Total built:		300,000 (approx.; all types)
Price, new:		$2,400 (1952)

Engine	Drawbar Hp	PTO/Belt Hp
5.5x6.5in	18.7	24.7
5.5x6.75in		
Kerosene	26.2	29.6
Gas	34.1	38

General Specifications

Engine displacement			
To serial number 498999			309ci
From serial number 499000			321ci
Engine rated rpm			975

Wheels and tires, standard

	Wheels	Tires
Rear	50x6in	11x38
Front	24x4	5.5x16

	Unstyled	1938–47	1947–52
Length	124in	133in	134in
Height to radiator	60in	62.5in	63.9in
Weight	3,525lb	3,783lb	4,909lb

Transmission

Speeds forward	
Early	4
After serial number 499000	6
Reverse	1

INTEGRAL EQUIPMENT

ONE-WAY PLOW.

TWO-WAY PLOW.

2-, 3-, or 4-ROW BEDDER.

TWO-ROW MIDDLEBREAKER.

TWO- OR FOUR-ROW BEDDER-PLANTER.

TWO-ROW LISTER.

1- OR 2-ROW DISK BEDDER.

TWO-ROW COTTON, CORN, PEANUT PLANTER. With or without fertilizer or pea attachment.)

TWO - ROW COMBINATION UNIT. (For bedding or furrowing planting and fertilizing once over.)

FOUR-ROW COTTON AND CORN PLANTER.

TWO-ROW CULTIVATORS,

ATTACHMENTS FOR TWO-ROW CULTIVATORS:

    TWO-ROW RUNNER-, SHOE-, OR SWEEP-TYPE PLANTING ATTACHMENTS.

    TWO-ROW FERTILIZER ATTACHMENT. (Used alone or with planting attachment.)

    TWO- OR FOUR-ROW BEAN HARVESTER ATTACHMENT.

    VARIABLE-ROW TOOL-BAR ATTACHMENTS. (For cultivating vegetables.)

    TWO-ROW PEANUT PULLER ATTACHMENTS.

TWO-ROW DISK CULTIVATOR.

TWO-ROW LISTED CORN CULTIVATORS.

FOUR-ROW CULTIVATORS.

FERTILIZER ATTACHMENT FOR FOUR-ROW CULTIVATORS.

VARIABLE - ROW CULTIVATORS. (For vegetables.)

TWO- OR FOUR-ROW BEAN HARVESTER ATTACHMENT. (For variable-row cultivators.)

COVER-CROP COMBINATION. (Consists of disk cultivator in front and middlebreaker in rear.)

DISK- AND BLADE-TYPE POTATO HOES.

SWEEP RAKES.

GRAIN SHOCK SWEEP.

ONE- AND TWO-ROW PUSH-TYPE CORN PICKERS.

TWO-ROW BEET LIFTER.

TWO- OR FOUR-ROW BEAN HARVESTER.

TWO-ROW PEANUT PULLER.

THE John Deere Model "A" is a new, more powerful tractor—a tractor that's been greatly improved, yet a tractor that has all of the features that have made John Deere General Purpose Tractors famous.

Built stronger throughout to match its increased horsepower and with an improved, more efficient engine to give even greater fuel economy, the new Model "A" handles more farm jobs under a wider variety of field and crop conditions, and at lower cost than ever before.

The new Model "A" pulls three 14-inch plow bottoms under average soil conditions in second gear, or two 16-inch plow bottoms in second or third gear; handles two- and four-row bedders, planters, cultivators; pulls and operates two-row corn pickers, field ensilage harvesters, power-driven combines; operates big-capacity, belt-driven machines with a greater power reserve; handles all these and many other heavy farm power jobs more efficiently and more economically.

It's the ideal tractor for farms where difficult soil conditions or hilly land demand greater power . . . for farms where more belt power is required . . . or for the large row-crop farms where big-capacity equipment is needed in order to farm at lowest cost and get the work done on time, ahead of bad weather, and when the field and crop conditions are right.

The styled Model A tractor from a 1941 Deere brochure. *Deere & Company*

The Model AO was constructed from 1936 to 1953 as an orchard tractor with the stack removed and the wheels shielded for working among citrus trees. *Deere & Company*

in 1933, the A, and a year later, the B, which replaced the GP.

At least eight experimental tractors were built before Deere settled on the configuration of the A, six of which incorporated the new four-speed transmission. The other two used the traditional three-speed unit. It is believed that these tractors, known as Models AA-1 and AA-3, were built in early 1933 and had serial numbers beginning with 410000. All eight experimental models were subsequently rebuilt in the A configuration and given new serial numbers or were scrapped.

The appearance of the new A and B models in the depth of the Depression rocked the

This Model AN was specifically designed for narrow-row crops.

competition on its heels and spoke volumes to the beleaguered farmers. The farmers, already in love with the rugged simplicity of Deere products and the performance of Deere tractors on low-cost kerosene, also bet their farms on the new tractors. The ability of these two tractors to deliver the goods for both the farmers and Deere accounts in part for their special endorsement by collectors. Like the lasting friendship of Foxhole buddies, a full bond developed between those who struggled with new tractors in the early thirties and the machines when they worked well.

Company literature of the time stated that the Model A had the pulling power of a six-horse team and had a daily work output greater than that of ten horses. A 1939 option of a generator and lights made night work practical, further exacerbating the horse-tractor disparity.

Model A Variations

The options of a single-front-wheel AN and adjustable axle, wide-front AW models

Model AR Specifications		
The following information generally applies to the AO and AI models as well:		
Years produced:		1935–1953
First serial number:		250000
Last serial number:		284074
Total built:		30,000 (approx.)
Price, new:		$2,300 (1951)
	Drawbar	**PTO/Belt**
Engine	**Hp**	**Hp**
5.5x6.5in		
Kerosene	18.7	24.7
Gas	34.9	39.1
General Specifications		
Engine displacement		
To serial number 259999		309ci
Late		321ci
Engine rated rpm		975
Tires, standard		
Rear		11.25x24
Front		6x16
Length		124in
Height to radiator		55in
Weight		3,400lb
Transmission		
Speeds forward		
To serial number 271999		4
After serial number 272000		6
Reverse		1

were added to the line for the 1935 crop season. The year 1937 saw the addition of the high-clearance versions, the ANH and the AWH, with 40in rear wheels rather than the usual 36in wheels. For the single-front-wheel version, the wheel size was increased from 10in to 16in. The wide-front version had extended front spindles. All high-clearance versions used pneumatic tires as original equipment and were not offered with steel wheels.

Also in 1935 came the Model AR—the standard-tread, or non-row-crop, tractor— the R designation standing for Regular tread. At this time, the general-purpose row-crop tractors were still considered aberrations of the regular Model D. Subsequent lowboy variants of models were given the submodel R designation, culminating in the ultimate

replacement for the D, the Model R, introduced in 1949.

Besides being lower than the Model A and heavier, at around 4,200lb, the Model AR did not have the adjustable wheel tread or the hydraulic lift of the Model A. The AR was also fitted with a single brake.

The Model AO was closely related to the AR. Changes included an undertractor exhaust, elimination of the vertical air pipe extension, and some minor sheet metal fairings. The Orchard version did regain the separate wheel brakes of the A, to assist in maneuvering among the trees.

The AR and the AO shared a serial numbering system separate from that of the rest of the A line, which began with 250000. Approximately 21,590 of these had been built when, in 1949, the styled AR and AO were

This Model AR is just about as nice as they come. The muffler should, however, be no taller than the intake pipe on an A. Replacement mufflers are longer than the originals. Some restorers carefully cut new ones off and reweld them.

brought out. These "new, improved" models had serial numbers beginning with 272000 and running to 284040, for about 12,040 total by mid-1953.

For 1936, a Model AOS (Streamlined) was added to the line-up. The AOS could well be called the first styled John Deere tractor, since its bodywork compared favorably with that of the Indianapolis 500 cars of the period. The AOS was produced through 1940 and used a separate serial numbering system, beginning with 1000, to prevent parts confusion with the AO.

Collecting Comments

The following is a chart of versions of the A by type, serial number, and year built. The star system investment rating is shown for each type. Note that the serial numbers for the non-general-purpose types follow a different sequence. Serial numbers for general-purpose tractors with the various front end configurations are intermingled. The only way to tell whether a tractor has its original front end configuration is by researching the serial number. The Two-Cylinder Club (see the "Sources" section near the end of this book) can assist in determining a tractor's original front end type, as can the Deere archives.

The regular, or standard-tread, A tractors were never produced in numbers like those of the row-crop versions, especially the later all-fuel AR and AO versions. Another rarity is an AR originally equipped with steel wheels. Note that AOs and ARs were produced until May of 1953.

Also note that although serial number sequences include thousands of numbers, only a very few numbers in the sequences are the four- and five-star tractors.

A Model AI. These rare versions of the A are among the most valuable of all the Deere collectibles. See the July–August 1990 issue of *Two-Cylinder* magazine for a write-up on the AI. *Deere & Company*

A nicely restored Model AO. Modifications necessary for it to push itself under low-hanging limbs can be clearly seen.

This Model A with an open fan shaft was purchased by Lyle Pals' father in 1934. When Pals went on his own, he bought the A from his dad. It's one of forty Deeres now owned by Pals and kept on his 2,000-acre spread near Leaf River, Illinois.

Serial Numbers and Year Models

The following chart provides a means of determining a tractor's year model. The number given is the first serial number of that year. Note that serial numbers were occasionally skipped so that a new version, or a new model year, could begin with an even number for ready recognition.

Year	Beginning Serial Number		
	A-GP	AO, AI, and AR	AOS
1934	410008		
1935	412869		
1936	424025	250000	
1937	442151	253521	AO-1000
1938	466787	255416	AO-1539
1939	477000	257004	AO-1725
1940	488000	258045	AO-1801
1941	499000	260000	
1942	514127	261558	
1943	523133	262243	
1944	528778	263223	
1945	548352	264738	
1946	555334	265870	
1947	578516	267082	
1948	594433	268877	
1949	620843	270646	
1950	648000	272985	
1951	667390	276078	
1952	689880	279770	
1953		282551	

The Model AOS was a Model A Orchard tractor with streamlined bodywork. Fewer than 900 were built between 1936 and 1940. *Reed Gerber*

Rating	Model	Years	Serial Numbers	Remarks
★★★★★	A	1934–1935	410008–414808	Open fan shaft 309ci engine
★★	A	1935–1938	414809–476999	
★★★★	AN, AW			
★★★★★	ANH, AWH	1937–1938	469668–476999	
★★	A	1938–1940	477000–498999	Styled, four-speed
★★★★	AN, AW			
★★★★★	ANH, AWH			
★★	A	1941–1947	499000–583999	Six-speed 321ci engine
★★★	AN, AW			
★★★★	ANH, AWH			
★★★	A	1947–1952	584000–703383	All-fuel engine Gasoline engine Pressed steel frame
★★				
★★★★	AN, AW, AH	1947–1952	584000–703383	All-fuel engine Gasoline engine
★★★				
★★★	AR	1935–1940		
★★★★★	AI	1936–1941	250000–259999	309ci engine Offset radiator cap
★★★★★	AO	1935–1936	250000–252723	Orchard
★★★	AR, AO	1941–1949	260000–271999	321ci engine Centered radiator cap
★★★★★	AOS	1936–1940	1000–1891	Streamlined Orchard
★★★	AR	1949–1953	272000–284074	Styled
★★★★★	AO			

The Model 60 was the first John Deere to give farmers a choice of a gasoline, all-fuel, or LPG engine. Constructed from 1952 to 1956, it was rated in 1952 at 27.71 drawbar hp and 35.33 belt hp, according to the State of Nebraska Test. *Deere & Company*

Model 60

The new Model 60 was introduced to dealers in June of 1952 as the successor to the great Model A. The A had been on the market for eighteen years, and during that period, it had been upgraded through four distinct versions:

Unstyled	(1934–1938)
Styled	four-speed, small engine (1938–1940)
Styled	six-speed, large engine (1941–1947)
Late styled	(1947–1952)

Each of these changes was evolutionary; the change to the 60 was revolutionary.

First, the new styling was like that of the beautiful Model R, introduced in 1949, with its squareish hood and wraparound pleated grille. Second, although the engine retained the same displacement and operating speed as those of the last A's engine, a host of

Model 60 Row-Crop Specifications

	Years produced:	1952–1956
	First serial number:	6000001
	Last serial number:	6063836
	Total built:	57,300 (approx.)
	Price, new:	$2,500 (1956)

Engine	Drawbar Hp	PTO/Belt Hp
Gasoline	36.9	41.6
Tractor fuel (improved kerosene-distillate fuel)	30.1	33.3
LPG	38.1	42.2

General Specifications	
Engine displacement	321ci
Engine bore and stroke	5.5x6.75in
Engine rated rpm	975
Tires, standard	
Rear	11x38
Front	6x16
Length	139in
Height to radiator	65.6in
Weight	5,300lb
Transmission	
Speeds forward	6
Reverse	1

Robert A. ("Tractor Bob") Hanson, who eventually became chairman of Deere, is plowing with a Model 60 tractor and 813 plow in this 1954 photo. This type of hands-on management accounts for a great deal of Deere's success. *Deere & Company*

A 1953 Model 60, showing off its vertical-pleat radiator cover. This is the type first introduced in 1949 on the Model R.

improvements gave it more power and more life.

Cyclonic fuel intake was the Madison Avenue term for a modified combustion chamber with a raised eyebrow over the intake valve to increase intake turbulence and fuel mixing. This, in conjunction with a two-barrel carburetor and a manually controlled intake manifold heat riser, provided for efficient vaporization and combustion of the fuel—be it gasoline, distillate, or liquefied petroleum gas (LPG), first offered in 1954.

A more conventional—by competitors' standards—cooling system was incorporated, using a pressurized radiator, a water pump, and thermostatically controlled radiator shutters. This replaced the traditional thermosyphon system, which had been a Deere trademark.

Two other new engine features for the 60 were positive crankcase ventilation, which prevented the formation of sludge by drawing clean air through the crankcase by means of an air pump, and an automatic fuel shutoff. The shutoff, controlled by engine oil pressure, served as a protective feature against operating without oil pressure. It also provided a positive shutoff to prevent fuel from flowing into the carburetor or engine with the tractor not running.

Other features of the new Model 60 included the following:
Live PTO
Live hydraulics and a preliminary type of three-point hitch
Easier steering and, in 1954, integral power steering
Simplified rear wheel adjustment
Optional rear exhaust
Two-piece pedestal permitting interchangeable front ends
Optional long axles and dished wheels for 104in spacing
12 volt electrical system

A Model 60 tractor maneuvers into close quarters carrying a two-bottom plow with its Yakima three-point hitch option. *Deere & Company*

Improved operator's seat
Lengthened clutch lever for easier operation
when standing

Model 60 Variations

The general-purpose row-crop version came with four interchangeable front end options: dual narrow front, dual narrow Roll-O-Matic front, wide front, and single wheel. The Model 60 was also available in Standard-Tread, Orchard, and Hi-Crop versions. All of these were available in gasoline, all-fuel, or LPG configurations.

The Hi-Crop was like the wide-front row-crop except higher. It provided a minimum of 32in of crop clearance. A special version of the Hi-Crop was equipped with a fixed 38in front axle for use with three-row bedder equipment.

The 60S (Standard-Tread) began life as a restyled and improved AR. This was known as the low-seat type. After serial number 6043000, the 60S was essentially a 60 row-crop with a straight front axle. This was known as the high-seat model.

The 60-O (Orchard) was basically a carry-over from the AO. It was unchanged from 1952 to mid-1957 when the 620 came out.

Collecting Comments

Following is a chart of versions of the 60. The star system investment rating is shown for each type. Note that although the serial numbers run consecutively through the years, the various versions are intermingled. This means that only a few of the four- and five-star versions were built and that they were randomly produced along with the more common types.

With almost 80 percent of the total Model 60 production having the dual conventional front end, or Roll-O-Matic, a lot of them are out there. Consequently, these do not fall into the unique category, and although they would qualify as antiques if they were automobiles, they are so modern and capable that they hardly fit that title. Nevertheless, the conventional Model 60 makes a fine collector tractor. Because of their convertibility, not as much credit can be given for the types with

YOUR CHOICE OF FRONT-END ASSEMBLIES

To match every job and crop requirement—provide maximum row-crop adaptability and general-purpose utility—John Deere "50," "60," and "70" Tractors are regularly equipped with a two-piece front pedestal that permits using any one of six interchangeable front-end assemblies.

You can choose Roll-O-Matic or conventional dual front wheels for working in normal-spaced rows . . . a single front wheel for narrow-spaced crops . . . a fixed 38-inch-tread front end for working 3-row bedders . . . or either of two adjustable front axles if your requirements call for four-wheel

stability and flotation or extreme tread adjustability for straddling beds or handling crops grown in wide-spaced rows.

You can order a John Deere "50," "60," or "70" Tractor equipped at the factory with the front-end assembly of your choice. If you have need for more than one type, you can purchase the additional equipment separately at any time. All assemblies are securely held in place by four cap screws and the change-over from one type to another is quick and simple. (For specifications see page 19.)

ROLL-O-MATIC   DUAL   SINGLE   38-INCH TREAD   ADJUSTABLE AXLES

A Deere brochure from 1951 spelling out the variety of front end configurations available on the new 50, 60, and 70 Models. *Deere & Company*

rarer front ends, anyway. Standard, Hi-Crop, Orchard, all-fuel, and LPG versions of the 60 are relatively scarce, and although collectors have generally driven the price of these up some, they do make excellent investments.

A well-restored 60 of any kind exhibits the best of John Deere, being the last of the all-green models, and is a pleasure to drive because of the comfortable seat and improved controls. The 60s, along with the 70s,

HI-CROP MODELS

Here are the tractors for growers of tall crops ... bushy crops ... bedded crops ... flowers ... sugar cane. They're the Models "60" and "70" Hi-Crops, available with gasoline, tractor fuel, or LP-Gas-burning engines. They offer all the features of the "60" and "70" Tractors plus more than 32 inches of clearance at every point under both front and rear axles, and a minimum of 45 inches between final drive housings. With these tractors you can get extra, damage-free cultivations that help produce better yields and bigger profits from tall-growing crops. A variety of special working equipment is available to handle high-clearance jobs.

The Hi-Crop version of the Model 60 and 70, as shown in a Deere brochure from 1951. *Deere & Company*

LONG REAR AXLES

Special long rear axles (shown at the right on the Model "50") are available if your conditions or crops call for extra rear wheel-tread adjustability. With these special axles and either a regular or offset wheel, tread adjustment is as follows.

Long Axles	"50"	"60"	"70"
Regular Wheel	62-98 inches		66-98 inches
Offset Wheel	56-104 inches		60-104 inches
Available in either 38- or 42-inch diameter.			

Extra long rear axles that permit tread adjustment from 66 to 105 inches with regular wheels and 60 to 112 inches with offset wheels are available for the "70."

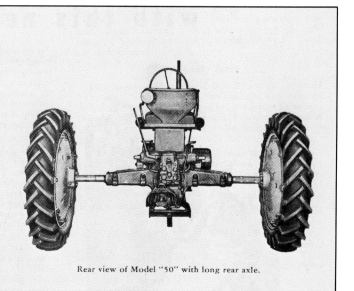

Rear view of Model "50" with long rear axle.

A Deere brochure from 1951 detailing the long rear axles available for regular and offset wheels on the Models 50, 60, and 70. *Deere & Company*

are also the last of the slow-turning (less-than-1000rpm) Deere two-cylinders. Once restored, owing to its inherent excess capacity, a 60 should not give its owner any trouble for the rest of time—except, perhaps, for the manual manifold temperature control, which is notorious for seizing up.

Serial Numbers and Year Models

The following chart provides a means of determining a tractor's year model:

Year	Beginning Serial Number
1952	6000001
1953	6007694
1954	6027995
1955	6042500
1956	6057650
1957	6063837

The last Model 60 was serial number 6064096, an LPG Orchard model, which was exported and is now unaccounted for.

Models 60S and 60-O Specifications

Years produced:		1952–1957
First serial number:		6000001
Last serial number:		6064096
Total built:		3,700 (approx.)
Price, new:		$2,550 (1956)

Engine	Drawbar Hp	PTO/Belt Hp
Gasoline	36.9	41.6
Tractor fuel	30.1	33.3
LPG	38.1	42.2

General Specifications

Engine displacement			321ci
Engine bore and stroke			5.5x6.75in
Engine rated rpm			975
Tires, standard			
Rear			14x30
Front			6x16

	Low-Seat	High-Seat	Orchard
Length	124in	127in	125in
Height to radiator	60in	66in	57in
Weight	4,350lb	6,175lb	5,330lb
Transmission			
Speeds forward			6
Reverse			1

The rare and beautiful 60 Orchard tractor. *Deere & Company*

Rating	Model	Years	Serial Numbers	Remarks
★★	60	1952–1956	6000001–6063836	Gasoline engine, dual front and Roll-O-Matic
★★★	60	1952–1956	6000001–6063836	Gasoline engine, wide front
★★★	60	1952–1956	6000001–6063836	Gasoline engine, single front wheel
★★★★	60	1952–1956	6000001–6063836	All-fuel engine, dual front and Roll-O-Matic
★★★★	60	1952–1956	6000001–6063836	All-fuel engine, wide front
★★★★	60	1952–1956	6000001–6063836	All-fuel engine, single front wheel
★★★★	60	1953–1956	6007694–6063836	LPG engine, dual front and Roll-O-Matic
★★★★	60	1953–1956	6007694–6063836	LPG engine, wide front
★★★★	60	1953–1956	6007694–6063836	LPG engine, single front wheel
★★★	60S	1952–1954	6000001–6042732	Gas engine, low seat
★★★★				All-fuel engine
★★★★★	60NS (New Style)	1954–1956	6027995–6063836	Gas engine, high seat
★★★★★				All-fuel engine
★★★★★				LPG engine
★★★★★	60-O	1952–1956	6000001–6063836	Gas engine
★★★★★				All-fuel engine
★★★★★		1956–1957	6063837–6064096	LPG engine
★★★★★	60 Hi-Crop	1952–1956	6000001–6063836	Gas engine
★★★★★				All-fuel engine
★★★★★				LPG engine

Model 620

The big news with the introduction of the 620 was the improved Custom Powr-Trol—Deere's version of Draft Control.

The three-point hitch with which the Model 60 could be equipped did not automatically compensate for changing soil conditions, as did the hitches of some of the competition. So, even though the new numbered series was only four years old, a redesign was ordered.

Along with Custom Powr-Trol came a 20 percent power increase through improved combustion chamber design and by means of a raise in rpm from 975 to 1125. These two features alone accounted for a considerable improvement in productivity of the 620 over the 60.

Another important feature of the 620 was the optional Power Rear Wheel Spacing. To change spacing, the operator loosened three clamps, set the stop to the desired place, and engaged the clutch, and engine power did the rest. The importance of this feature to some farmers cannot be overstated. In some cases, it allowed a farmer to get by with one, rather than two, tractors.

Although styling was basically unchanged between the 60 and the 620, a new paint scheme was used, with yellow panels along the hood sides. The optional Float-Ride seat improved operator comfort.

Model 620 Row-Crop Specifications		
Years produced:		1956–1958
First serial number:		6200000
Last serial number:		6222686
Total built:		22,500 (approx.)
Price, new:		$3,200 (1958)
	Drawbar	PTO/Belt
Engine	Hp	Hp
Gasoline	44.2	48.7
Tractor fuel	32.7	35.7
LPG	45.8	50.3
General Specifications		
Engine displacement		321ci
Engine bore and stroke		5.5x6.75in
Engine rated rpm		1125
Tires, standard		
Rear		12.4x38
Front		6x16
Length		135.25in
Height to radiator		66in
Weight		5,900lb
Transmission		
Speeds forward		6
Reverse		1

Models 620S and 620-O Specifications		
Years produced:		1956–1960
First serial number:		6200000
Last serial number:		6223247
Total built:		3,000 (approx.)
Price, new:		$3,500 (1958)
	Drawbar	PTO/Belt
Engine	Hp	Hp
Gasoline	44.2	48.7
Tractor fuel	32.7	35.7
LPG	45.8	50.3
General Specifications		
Engine displacement		321ci
Engine bore and stroke		5.5x6.75in
Engine rated rpm		1125
Tires, standard		
Rear		
Standard-Tread		13x30
Orchard (grove)		14x26
Front		6x16
	Standard	Orchard
Length	127in	126in
Height to radiator	66in	57in
Weight	6,480lb	6,350lb
Transmission		
Speeds forward		6
Reverse		1

Model 620 Variations

The general-purpose row-crop version came with four interchangeable front end options: dual narrow front, dual narrow Roll-O-Matic front, wide front, and single wheel. Standard-Tread, Orchard, and Hi-Crop versions were also available. All types came in gasoline, all-fuel, or LPG configurations. The 620H (Hi-Crop) was like the wide-front row-

The Model 620 was part of the 20 Series that replaced the Model 60 in 1956 and continued to be offered through 1958. It was rated at 34.34 drawbar hp and 42.79 belt hp, according to the State of Nebraska Test. *Deere & Company*

All 620 Orchard models are quite rare, but LPG types, as shown here, are even more rare. *Deere & Company*

Rating	Model	Years	Serial Numbers	Remarks
★★	620	1956–1958	6200000–6222686	Gasoline engine, dual front and Roll-O-Matic
★★★	620	1956–1958	6200000–6222686	Gasoline engine, wide front
★★★★	620	1956–1958	6200000–6222686	Gasoline engine, single front wheel
★★★★	620	1956–1958	6200000–6222686	All-fuel engine, dual front and Roll-O-Matic
★★★★	620	1956–1958	6200000–6222686	All-fuel engine, wide front
★★★★★	620	1956–1958	6200000–6222686	All-fuel engine, single front wheel
★★★★	620	1956–1958	6200000–6222686	LPG engine, dual front and Roll-O-Matic
★★★★	620	1956–1958	6200000–6222686	LPG engine, wide front
★★★★	620	1956–1958	6200000–6222686	LPG engine, single front wheel
★★★★★	620H	1956–1958	6201868–6208055	Gas, LPG, or all-fuel engine
★★★★	620S	1956–1957	6200195–6208866	Gas, LPG, or all-fuel engine
★★★★★	620-O	1957–1960	6203778–6223247	Gas, LPG, or all-fuel engine

crop except higher, providing a minimum of 32in of crop clearance. The 620S (Standard-Tread) was essentially a 620 row-crop with a straight front axle.

The 620-O (Orchard) was basically a carry-over from the AO and 60-O, which remained unchanged through mid-1957 when the 620-O came out. At that time, it received changes and the yellow paint panels common to the rest of the 20 Series. The 620-O was the last two-cylinder Orchard tractor. Its production continued until February 1960.

Collecting Comments

Although accounting for more than 80 percent of 620 production, the conventional row-crops were still not made in as high numbers as previous big mama tractors were. Hi-Crop, Standard-Tread, and Orchard versions are rare, as are all-fuel and LPG models. Wide-front and narrow-front (single-front-wheel) variations of the row-crops are relatively rare, but their ready convertibility and lack of factory configura-tion records prevent them from achieving their full potential as collectibles.

Following is a chart of versions of the 620. The star system investment rating is shown for each type.

Serial Numbers and Year Models

The following chart provides a means of determining a tractor's year model:

Year	Beginning Serial Number
1956	6200000
1957	6203778
1958	6215048

Model 630

In August of 1958, dealers began to receive the new 630, successor to the 620. The big mama 630 was considered to be a heavy-duty four-plow machine. This meant, according to Deere literature, that it had the power to handle large-acreage farms. What the writers had in mind, besides a four-bottom plow, was a six-row planter or a six-row cultivator.

The Model 630 made its debut with the 30 Series as a replacement for the 20 Series, with an emphasis on more power and operator convenience and comfort. Introduced in 1958, it continued in production into 1961. It was advertised at 44.16 drawbar hp and 48.68 belt hp. *Deere & Company*

Although the power of the 630 was the same as that of the 620, productivity improved through improved ergonomics—the science of improving workstation comfort and convenience. For example, the new-style flat-top fenders offered convenient handholds for mounting and dismounting. They also housed an improved four-light lighting system for better night vision. These fender functions were in addition to protecting the

Model 630 Row-Crop Specifications		
Years produced:		1958–1960
First serial number:		6300000
Last serial number:		6318206
Total built:		18,000 (approx.)
Price, new:		$3,300 (1958)
	Drawbar	PTO/Belt
Engine	**Hp**	**Hp**
Gasoline	44.2	48.7
Tractor fuel	32.7	35.7
LPG	45.8	50.3
General Specifications		
Engine displacement		321ci
Engine bore and stroke		5.5x6.75in
Engine rated rpm		1125
Tires, standard		
Rear		12.4x38
Front		6x16
Length		135.25in
Height to radiator		66in
Weight		5,900lb
Transmission		
Speeds forward		6
Reverse		1

Model 630S Specifications		
Years produced:		1958–1960
First serial number:		6300088
Last serial number:		6317201
Total built:		2,000 (approx.)
Price, new:		$3,450
	Drawbar	PTO/Belt
Engine	**Hp**	**Hp**
Gasoline	44.2	48.7
Tractor fuel	32.7	35.7
LPG	45.8	50.3
General Specifications		
Engine displacement		321ci
Engine bore and stroke		5.5x6.75in
Engine rated rpm		1125
Tires, standard		
Rear, standard tread		13x30
Front		6x16
Length		127in
Height to radiator		66in
Weight		6,480lb
Transmission		
Speeds forward		6
Reverse		1

operator from dust or mud. Other ergonomic improvements included the following:

● A new deep-cushioned adjustable seat with a cushioned backrest
● A redesigned steering mechanism with the steering wheel at a more convenient and comfortable angle
● A redesigned, easy-to-read instrument panel with instruments clustered around the steering wheel
● A new low-tone oval muffler to be even easier on the ears

Styling remained the same, except that the cowl was changed to allow the new steering wheel position. Sheet metal paint, trim, and lettering were somewhat different from those on the 620.

Model 630 Variations

The general-purpose row-crop 630 came with four interchangeable front end options: dual narrow front, dual narrow Roll-O-Matic front, wide front, and single wheel. 630S (Standard-Tread) and 630H (Hi-Crop) versions were also available. All types came in gasoline, all-fuel, or LPG configurations. The Model 620-O, or grove, tractor continued in production; no 630 Orchard model was offered.

Collecting Comments

Although the 630 is over thirty years old, its power and capability make it still much in demand by farmers for routine farm chores. A new 40hp to 50hp tractor would cost three

A 630 Wide Front cultivates six rows of corn with a Number 62 cultivator. Note the comfortable seating position and convenient controls that characterized the 30 Series tractors. *Deere & Company*

Rating	Model	Years	Serial Numbers	Remarks
★★	630	1958–1960	6300000–6318206	Gasoline engine, dual front and Roll-O-Matic
★★★	630	1958–1960	6300000–6318206	Gasoline engine, wide front
★★★	630	1958–1960	6300000–6318206	Gasoline engine, single front wheel
★★★	630	1958–1960	6300000–6318206	All-fuel engine, dual front and Roll-O-Matic
★★★★	630	1958–1960	6300000–6318206	All-fuel engine, wide front
★★★★	630	1958–1960	6300000–6318206	All-fuel engine, single front wheel
★★★★	630	1958–1960	6300000–6318206	LPG engine, dual front and Roll-O-Matic
★★★★	630	1958–1960	6300000–6318206	LPG engine, wide front
★★★★	630	1958–1960	6300000–6318206	LPG engine, single front wheel
★★★★★	630H	1958–1960	6300687–6315983	Gas, LPG, or all-fuel engine
★★★★★	630S	1958–1960	6300088–6317201	Gas, LPG, or all-fuel engine

to four times as much as a good, refurbished 630, although the new one would be a diesel and would probably have a transmission with power shift, shuttle reverse or both. Nevertheless, for many jobs around the farm, a 630 would be just fine. As a collector tractor, however, its demand by farmers is keeping the prices higher than for other thirty-year-old tractors of lesser capabilities.

All-fuel and LPG versions of the 630 are rare, as are Standard-Tread versions and the Hi-Crop model. If you have, for example, a Hi-Crop LPG tractor, you have a fairly valuable commodity. More than 70 percent of 630s were dual narrow-fronts, or Roll-O-

Matics, but these were readily converted to single-wheel-fronts or wide-fronts. Since factory build configurations were not recorded, little credit can be given for these types in the star ratings that follow.

Serial Numbers and Year Models

The following chart provides a means of determining a tractor's year model:

Year	Beginning Serial Number
1958	6300000
1959	6302749
1960	6314381

Chapter 7

John Deere Models C, GP, B, 50, 520, and 530

Little Brother

By the mid-twenties, Deere had firmly established itself as a viable tractor maker. Although it was experiencing fierce competition from Ford and International Harvester, the strongest competitor was still the horse. The powerful standard-tread Model D was generally considered a plowing tractor or a

prime mover engine for the thresher, performing jobs that the steam traction engine had long since taken over from the horse. But times were changing. Most day-to-day farm work was done using a team of two horses. Thus, a need was recognized for a tractor smaller than the D—and later the A—for

An early experimental tractor. Development of a general-purpose row-crop tractor began where efforts to build a motor cultivator left off. It occurred in three distinct phases. First, five experimental tractors were built in 1926, followed by twenty-four more in 1927. Next, seventy-five upgraded versions that carried the Model C designation were built. These were all given numbers between 200000

and 200110. Finally, field problems resulted in the recall of the Cs, and fifty-two of them were rebuilt. Along with these, twenty-three new tractors were built. The resulting seventy-five were numbered beginning with 200111. Model Cs were replaced in 1928 by the GP, a tractor with minor improvements, beginning with serial number 200211. *Deere & Company*

POWER FARMING WITH GREATER PROFIT

One Hundred Years Ago JOHN DEERE GAVE TO THE WORLD THE STEEL PLOW

John Deere Model B General Purpose

THE John Deere Model B General Purpose is proving the ideal power unit for operators of relatively small, general farms where the power requirements are not great enough to employ a tractor of larger size. It is adaptable to do all manner of work that a small tractor would be called upon to do, including all kinds of planting and cultivating in row crops, even to truck gardening.

Another group of larger farm operators, already using large tractors, are adding John Deere Model B Tractors to do some of the lighter, miscellaneous operations that are not so well adapted to the large tractor. These farms can utilize the two tractors to advantage because there is plenty of work for both.

All the Modern Features

The Model B is about two-thirds the size of the Model A in power and weight, but has all of the advanced John Deere General-Purpose features . . . adjustable tread . . . four forward speeds . . . narrow, compact design . . . light weight. It is a revelation in its bed-rock economy of operation . . . its amazing ease of handling.

It is a general purpose tractor in every sense of the word, with all that the name "John Deere" on tractors means . . . simplicity . . . quality construction . . . dependability . . . easy access to all parts . . . easy to keep in good running order.

Like the Model A, the Model B is equipped with power shaft for operating power take-off machines and can be equipped with hydraulic power lift for raising and lowering power-lifted working equipment.

It is big in power for its size—will handle the load ordinarily pulled by 4 horses on drawbar jobs.

It's the Tractor Farmers Wanted

The design and construction of this new tractor represent the mature and composite judgment of practical farmers—men who have had years of experience in the practical operation of tractors—men who are in position to make recommendations that are of real value.

The view at the top of the page shows the Model B equipped with regular solid-tired steel rear wheels with 4-inch spade lugs. The small views, below, show how this versatile John Deere tractor can be adapted to meet particular farming needs.

Rubber Tires

The Model B can be furnished with special rear wheels and 9.00 x 36″ or 7.50 x 36″ low-pressure rubber tires and tubes; special front wheels with 5.00 x 15″ low-pressure tires and tubes.

Skeleton Wheels

The Model B is shown at the right equipped with skeleton-type rear wheels—favorite equipment in many sections where the soil is firm or hard.

The unstyled Model B general-purpose tractor as featured in the John Deere *Power Farming With* *Greater Profit* pamphlet produced in 1937. *Deere & Company*

Deere's General Purpose tractor was aptly named when it was introduced in 1928 as a replacement for the farmer's draft horses. Constructed through 1935, the GP was also available in an early Orchard version. In 1928, the GP was rated at 10 drawbar hp and 20 belt hp as a kerosene burner. By 1931, it was up to 15.52 drawbar hp and 24.3 belt hp, according to the State of Nebraska Test. *Deere & Company*

The GPWT with its final-version overhead steering. The transverse implement mounting holes, behind the front wheels, are characteristic of the GPWT. *Reed Gerber*

such work as could be done by a horse team, and because a tractor doesn't tire, it could actually replace four to six horses.

International Harvester was flooding the market with the new Farmall in 1926, billing it as a general-purpose tractor. It could be used for planting, cultivating, and harvesting, as well as for plowing and for driving the thresher. This was revolutionary and a real challenge to the horse. In response to the Farmall, Deere brought out the 10 drawbar hp Model GP. It was about two-thirds the power and weight of the D. This size niche proved to be popular, even after the horse had been well replaced, and the little brother series of tractors turned out to be the largest selling in the Deere line-up.

Model GP

The GP was introduced in 1928 and was the second production tractor to bear the John Deere name. It had the same basic layout as the Model D, but, because it was designed as

Model GP Specifications

	Years produced:	1928–1935
	First serial number:	200211
	Last serial number:	230745
	Total built:	30,534 (approx.)
	Price, new:	$800 (1928); $1,200 (1931)

Engine	Drawbar Hp	PTO/Belt Hp
5.75x6in	10	20
6x6in	16	24

General Specifications

Engine displacement	
Early	312ci
Late	339ci
Engine rated rpm	950
Wheels, standard	
Rear	42x10
Front	24x6
Length	112in
Width	60in
Height to radiator	56in
Weight	3,600lb
Transmission	
Speeds forward	3
Reverse	1

A like-new Model GP on the showroom floor at Deere World Headquarters.

a three-row row-crop tractor, it was immediately distinguished from the D by the high arched front axle, designed to straddle the middle row.

The GP featured a mechanical implement power lift system—an industry first—and individual rear wheel brakes. It also incorporated a 520rpm PTO and several custom-designed implements. It and the L and LA Series are the only Deere tractors to use a side-valve L-head engine.

Although the GP continued in the line until 1935, its acceptance by farmers, especially in the South, and its performance in the field were somewhat disappointing. Acceptance was low primarily because of the three-row concept. Farmers wanted two-row equipment in some areas and four-row in others. In addition, the $800 price tag was high for a 10hp tractor, with the Farmall selling for around $600. The GP should have had more horsepower, but Deere engineers could not get the engine to come up to expectations until late 1930, when the bore was increased 0.25in.

Nevertheless, the GP was a fine, hardworking, long-lived tractor that today is highly prized by John Deere collectors.

The John Deere Model GP actually began life as the Model C, but after 110 production units were built, the designation was changed to better counter that of the general-purpose Farmall and because C sounded too much like D. One must remember that the quality of the telephone system of the late twenties was nothing like that of today, and if dealers ordered parts for a D from the factory, they didn't want to receive parts for a C.

Model GP Variations

During the experiments associated with the Model C, one configuration that was tried used a tricycle layout; that is, it had two front wheels close together and the rear wheels on a 50in tread. As soon as it was recognized that the three-row layout of the standard GP was not being accepted in all quarters, a tricycle GP was brought out with the same arrangement. About twenty-three of these were interspersed in the GP production during late 1929 and early 1930. At least two had special rear treads of 68in to accommodate two standard potato rows.

Later in 1929, the GPWT (Wide-Tread) was introduced. It had longer axles, giving it a 76in rear tread, allowing it to straddle two 42in rows. In 1930, some 203 were built with the special potato axles and wheels, all but one of which were delivered to the state of Maine; the remaining one was kept by the

77

The GPO was Deere's first orchard tractor. Notice the molded hard rubber tires. *Deere & Company*

Deere Experimental Department. In 1931, special dished wheels were developed, allowing the standard Wide-Tread to be convertible to potato rows, and the GP-P Series was eliminated. In 1932, the hood of the GPWT was narrowed for better vision and the steering was changed to use a shaft running over the engine.

The first John Deere Orchard tractor was based on the GP. It had fender skirts covering the rear wheels down to below the hubs and extending over the flywheel and belt pulley. Thus, the GPO (Orchard) came out in 1930. Some examples—the exact number is not known—were purchased by the Lindeman Company of Yakima, Washington, and were

Rating	Model	Years	Serial Numbers	Remarks
★★★	GP	1928–1930	200211–223802	Arched front axle 5.75 × 6in engine
★★★	GP	1930–1935	223803–230745	6 × 6in engine
★★★★★	GP Tricycle	1928–1929	200264–204213	Only 23 built, interspersed in these serial numbers
★★★★	GPO	1931–1935	15000–15732	
★★★★	GPWT	1929–1930	400000–402039	5.75 × 6in engine
★★★★		1930–1932	402040–404809	6 × 6in engine
★★★★		1932–1933	404810–405252	Overhead steering
★★★★★	GP-P	1930	5000–5202	5.75 × 6in engine 68in rear tread

fitted with crawler tracks for use in the large, hilly western apple orchards. Eleven of these Lindeman GPOs were known to exist in 1992.

Collecting Comments

Following is a chart of versions of the GP by type, serial number, and year built. The star system investment rating is shown for each type. Note that the serial numbers generally run consecutively through the year but that the various versions and types were sometimes intermingled.

It is believed that all remaining original Model Cs are in the hands of collectors, and a rating of only five stars hardly does them justice. They were given serial numbers 200111 to 200202 and have Model C on the nameplate. Experimental Model C serial number 200109 is known to exist; 200108 may also exist.

Serial Numbers and Year Models

The following chart provides a means of determining a tractor's year model. The GP's model year generally started in August of the preceding calendar year, except for the GP-O series, which started in November.

	Beginning Serial Number		
Year	Standard	Wide-Tread	Orchard
1928	200111		
1929	202566	400000	
1930	216139	400936	
1931	224321	402741	15000
1932	228666	404770	15226
1933	229051	405110	15387
1934	229216		15412
1935	230515		15589

Model B

The Model B has the distinction of being the best-selling tractor model produced by Deere, with well over 300,000 delivered. It was designed more or less simultaneously with the A, although the A was introduced in 1934 whereas the B was delayed until Model year 1935. The B incorporated all the advances of the A, such as the hydraulic implement lift, adjustable rear wheel tread, and one-piece rear axle housing. In fact, it was roughly a two-thirds scale model of the A in both size and power, a relationship that had proved successful with the Models D and GP.

The B was needed in large part because by 1935 the power of the GP was approaching

The Model B was introduced in 1935 as a smaller version of Deere's great Model A and was built through 1952. In 1935, it was rated at 9.28 drawbar hp and 14.25 belt hp, according to the State of Nebraska Test. *Deere & Company*

Fourteen-year-old Jim Borski of Van Dyne, Wisconsin, puts his 1937 Model B to the belt, driving a 32x54 Minneapolis thresher. Borski, who restored the tractor himself—with a little help from his dad and brother—was pleased with how the B did with such a load. It pulled it well, he said, as long as they didn't feed the bundles too fast.

that of the new Model A and a new, smaller, more agile tractor was needed to compete with a team of horses. The Model B filled a niche not only because of its smaller size, but also because it cost less and took less fuel than larger tractors, including the GP it replaced. Nebraska Tractor Test number 232 showed the B producing a little over 10 horsepower-hours per gallon of low-cost kerosene—an improvement of about 1 horsepower-hour per gallon over the GP.

John Deere Models A and B were both productions of the fertile mind of Theo Brown, a Deere engineering team leader. In late 1932, when Brown and his team began work on the new tractors, the general-purpose row-crop tractor had come into its own. By then, it was clear that a market existed for both row-crops and standard-tread tractors. It also had developed that the tricycle config-

The pressed steel frame rails of this Model B mean it is a 1947 or later model.

THE

B

INTEGRAL EQUIPMENT

ONE-WAY PLOW.

TWO-WAY PLOW.

ONE-, TWO-, OR THREE-ROW BEDDER.

TWO-ROW MIDDLEBREAKER.

TWO-ROW BEDDER-PLANTER.

TWO-ROW LISTER.

TWO-ROW COTTON, CORN, AND PEANUT PLANTER. (Available with or without fertilizer or pea attachment.)

TWO-ROW COMBINATION UNIT. (For bedding or furrowing, planting and fertilizing in one operation.)

TWO-ROW CULTIVATORS.

ATTACHMENTS FOR TWO-ROW CULTIVATORS:

TWO-ROW RUNNER-, SHOE-, OR SWEEP-TYPE PLANTING ATTACHMENT.

TWO-ROW FERTILIZER ATTACHMENT. (Used alone or with planting attachment.)

VARIABLE - ROW TOOL - BAR ATTACHMENT. (For cultivating beets, beans and other vegetables.)

TWO- OR FOUR-ROW BEAN HARVESTER ATTACHMENT.

TWO-ROW PEANUT PULLER ATTACHMENT.

TWO-ROW DISK CULTIVATORS.

TWO-ROW LISTED CORN CULTIVATORS.

VARIABLE-ROW CULTIVATORS. (For beets, beans, and other vegetables.)

TWO- OR FOUR-ROW BEAN HARVESTER ATTACHMENT. (For variable-row cultivators.)

TWO-ROW DISK- AND BLADE-TYPE POTATO HOES.

TWO- OR FOUR-ROW BEAN HARVESTER.

TWO-ROW BEET LIFTER.

ONE-ROW PUSH-TYPE CORN PICKER.

TWO-ROW PEANUT PULLER.

SWEEP RAKES.

THE John Deere Model "B" is the ideal tractor for farms where the power requirements are not great enough to justify the purchase of the larger Model "A" or "G". It is also ideal for use as supplementary power on farms of considerable acreage where a larger tractor is already in use.

The new Model "B" delivers 4-way power through drawbar, belt, power take-off, and power lift. Handles two 14-inch plow bottoms or a two-bottom bedder in average soil conditions, and gives you the daily work output of six to eight horses. It is adaptable to all farm jobs within its power range—pulls plows, listers, disk harrows, and other implements . . . operates belt-driven machines . . . pulls and operates power take-off machines such as corn pickers, small combines, mowers, grain binders, and many others . . . and furnishes power through a hydraulic lift for raising and lowering the wide variety of available integral equipment such as two-row planters, bedders, listers, and cultivators, hay tools, harvesting equipment, etc.

The Model "B" has four forward speeds—there's one for every job from plowing in heavy soil to hauling on the open road. Full adjustability of the rear wheels enables you to handle all row crops.

The styled Model B tractor from a 1941 Deere brochure. *Deere & Company*

A late, styled Model B, viewed from the flywheel side.

The steering wheel of this late, styled Model B is a John Deere current replacement part. The original had rod spokes. The owner is having the original wheel restored.

A late, styled Model B with Roll-O-Matic front. To provide the necessary clearance for the action of the front wheels, Roll-O-Matic tractors sit with their front end higher than level. The high part of the pressed steel frame on an A extends farther forward and is noticeably higher.

uration was the conventional arrangement for such machines, and, except for certain specialized applications, the new GPs—as As and Bs were called—would vastly outsell the standard-tread tractors such as the Model D.

The A was introduced first simply because of the limitations of human resources and facilities. Besides designing and testing the new line, Brown and his staff still had responsibility for the original Model GP and its variations, so it was almost a year after the debut of the A that the B reached the dealers. The B was originally available with pneumatic tires—the A was not—and it had a four-speed transmission, a PTO, and a belt

A late, styled Model B, showing the slim lines as created by industrial designer Henry Dreyfuss.

Some interesting characteristics of the John Deere tractor: The hydraulics and rock shaft are in a built-up unit on the back of the tractor. A toggle holds the left (parking) brake in the actuated position. The complicated shift gate shown here was used on later six-speed transmissions. The box beneath the seat is the battery box. The seat slides back and forth on the channels above the battery box.

A nice 1941 Model B, parked in the front yard to attract a buyer.

The Model BO was constructed from 1936 to 1947 as an orchard tractor with covered fenders to protect low-hanging citrus tree branches. *Deere & Company*

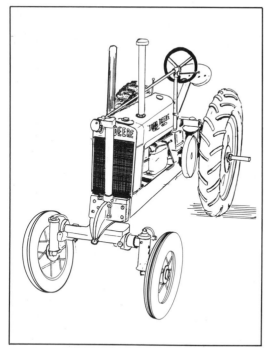

The Model BW-40, a special narrow version of the B, was built for vegetable work. It could straddle 40in beds of beets or two 20in rows of other vegetables. Records indicate that only six were made. *Reed Gerber*

Model B Row-Crop Specifications

Years produced:		1935–1952
First serial number:		1000
Last serial number:		310775
Total built:		300,000 + (all types)
Price, new:		$1,900 (1952)

Engine	Drawbar Hp	PTO/Belt Hp
4.25x5.25in	11.8	16
4.5x5.5in	14	18.5
4.69x5.5in		
Kerosene	21.1	23.5
Gas	24.6	27.6

General Specifications

Engine displacement			
To serial number 59999			149ci
To serial number 200999			175ci
To serial number 310775			190ci
Engine rated rpm			
To serial number 200999			1150
After serial number 201000			1250

Wheels and tires, standard	Wheels	Tires
Rear	48x5.25in	10x38
Front	22x3.25in	5.5x16

	Unstyled	1938–47	1947–52
Length	120.5in	125.5in	132.3in
Height to radiator	56in	57in	59.6in
Weight	2,760lb	2,880lb	4,000lb

Transmission	
Speeds forward	
Early	4
After serial number 96000	6
Reverse	1

pulley. Its engine, a scaled version of that in the A, had enough power for one 16in plow; the A was capable of pulling two 14s.

Model B Variations

The Model B came in so many variations that although total production was high, many opportunities exist for the collector to pick up a fairly unique type. For purposes of definition, the B falls into four distinct groups:

General purpose, unstyled   (1935–1938)
General purpose, styled   (1939–1946)
General purpose, late styled (1947–1952)
Standard-tread, unstyled   (1935–1947)

Within the general-purpose ranks are the B, BN, BW, BNH, and BWH variations. A further variation in the front end arrangement is that the first tractors built in 1935— serial numbers 1000 to 3042—used four at-

This early, styled BNH sports a round-spoke single front wheel.

An early, styled Model BNH with extra-wide vegetable rear axle shafts, some nice round-spoke wheels, and some old-tread rear tires.

SPECIAL EQUIPMENT

IN ADDITION to the starting and lighting equipment for the Models "A" and "B", shown on the previous page, John Deere General Purpose Tractors are available with a wide variety of other special equipment that adapts them to every requirement.

Rubber Tires

The table below shows sizes of rubber tires available for John Deere General Purpose Tractors.

	Tire Size	Ply	Wheel Equipment
Model "A"	9–38	4	Steel-Disk Type
Model "A"	9–38	6	Steel-Disk and Heavy-Cast Types
Model "A"	10–38	4 and 6	Steel-Disk and Heavy-Cast Types
Model "A"	11–38	6	Heavy-Cast Type
Model "B"	8–38	4 and 6	Steel-Disk and Heavy-Cast Types
Model "B"	9–38	4 and 6	Steel-Disk and Heavy-Cast Types
Model "G"	10.00 x 36	6	Spoke- and Heavy-Cast Types
Model "G"	11.25 x 36	6	Spoke- and Heavy-Cast Types

A variety of wheel weights is available to secure maximum traction under varying soil conditions when tractors are equipped with rubber tires.

Hydraulic Power Lift

Hydraulic power lift, as shown and described on page 12, is available for Models "A", "B", and "G" Tractors as special equipment.

Fenders

The illustration below shows the fender equipment available for Models "A", "B", and "G" Tractors.

A wide variety of equipment is also available for John Deere General Purpose Tractors mounted on steel wheels.

Lug equipment includes spade lugs for use in abrasive soils; A-shaped lugs for rough and rocky ground; button lugs and cast cone lugs for hayfield work; sand lugs for very sandy soils; and spud lugs for golf course work.

Extension rims for front and rear wheels, guide bands, road band assemblies, and front and rear wheel scrapers can also be furnished.

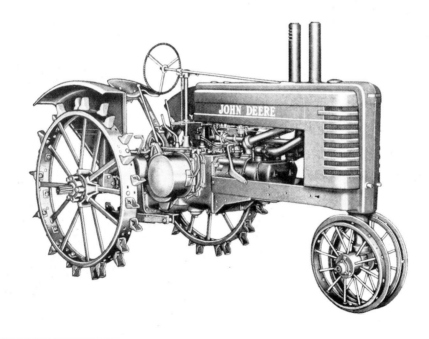

Special equipment was available in the 1940s for the Models A, B, and G, including rubber tires, a hydraulic power lift, and rear fenders. *Deere & Company*

tach bolts for the pedestal; after serial number 3042, an eight-bolt pedestal was used. These variations are known to collectors as four-bolt and eight-bolt tractors.

The original B, until serial number 42133, had a shorter frame by approximately 5in than that of subsequent unstyled models. The additional length allowed the use of the same mounted cultivators on both the A and the B. No tractors used serial numbers 42134 to 42199 so that long-frame models could begin with an even number. Serial numbers 42200 and up are known as long-hood, or long-frame, types by collectors.

The BN single-front-wheel and BW wide-front arrangements were available options from the beginning. In 1937, the high-clearance versions, BNH and BWH, were announced, along with similar models of the A.

Two versions of the B were designed especially for vegetable growers. The first, called the Garden Tractor, had a single front wheel and narrower rubber back tires. The second, called the BW-40, had especially shortened axle housings, allowing 40in minimum wheel spacing front and back, for tilling bedded crops, such as beets. Records indicate that only six BW-40s were sold, so they are extremely valuable to collectors.

By the end of 1935, three more closely related variations were announced: the BR lowboy, as opposed to the tricycle row-crop; the BI (Industrial), which was similar except it was yellow and had frame pads for mounting industrial equipment, an underneath exhaust, and an armchair seat; and the BO, which had optional extended rear fenders, underhood air intake, and a regular seat.

A 1952 Model BW residing in a forest of other John Deere tractors. Note the pressed steel frame, characteristic of late, styled Bs and As.

This Model BO Lindeman Crawler was built for orchard work in the West. The tractor, less running gear, was delivered to Lindeman's Yakima plant, where these tracks were installed. This is one of 2,000 made between 1939 and 1947.

A front pulley-side view of a Model BO Lindeman Crawler shows the orchard muffler just above and to the right of the belt pulley.

Model BR Specifications

The following information generally applies to the BO and BI models as well:

Years produced:	1935–1947
First serial number:	325000
Last serial number:	337514
Total built:	12,514 (approx.; includes 2,000 Lindemans)
Price, new:	$2,000 (1947)

Engine	Drawbar Hp	PTO/Belt Hp
4.25x5.25in	9.3	14.3
4.5x5.5in	13.8	17.5

General Specifications

Engine displacement	
To serial number 328999	149ci
Late	175ci
Engine rated rpm	1150
Tires, standard	
Rear	9x28
Front	5.5x16
Length	117.7in
Height to radiator	50.5in
Weight	3,375lb
Transmission	
Speeds forward	4
Reverse	1

Rating	Model	Years	Serial Numbers	Remarks
★★★	B-GP	1935–1937	1000-42199	Short hood
★★★★	BN, BW			149ci engine
★★★	B-GP	1937–1938	42200–59999	Long hood
★★★★	BN, BW			
★★★★★	BNH, BWH		46175–59999	
★★	B-GP	1938–1940	60000–95999	Styled, four-speed
★★★	BN, BW			175ci engine
★★★★★	BNH, BWH			
★★	B-GP	1941–1947	96000–200999	Same styling as in
★★★	BN, BW			1938–1940, six-speed
★★★★	BNH, BWH			
★★	B-GP	1947–1952	201000–310775	Late styled
★★★	BN, BW			Pressed steel frame 190ci engine
★★★★★	BR, BO	1935–1938	325000–328999	149ci engine
★★★★★	BR, BO	1938–1947	329000–337514	175ci engine
★★★★★	BI	1936–1941	325617–332157	Serial numbers interspersed with those of the BR and BO
★★★★★	BO	1939–1947	329000–337514	Lindeman Crawler 2,000 made—serial numbers interspersed with those of the BO and BN

None of these versions had adjustable wheel spacing or hydraulics, and only the BO had individual wheel brakes.

All B variations before 1941 used a four-speed transmission. Row-crop versions, serial numbers 96000 and up, were equipped with a six-speed gearbox.

Three engine displacements were used on the Model B: 149ci, 175ci, and 190ci. The stroke remained the same, but the bore was increased, first in 1938 when the B row-crops were styled and then again in 1947 when the pressed steel frame replaced the angle iron type. The BI model was discontinued in 1941, so it got only the first displacement increase, as did the BR and BO models, which were discontinued in 1947.

The Models A and B row-crops were the first to receive the Dreyfuss design treatment. The lowboy B models—the BR, BO, and BI—were never styled, being discon-

Some clever angles are incorporated into the various levers for controlling the Model BO Lindeman to avoid interference. The tall lever to the right is the hand-operated clutch, which you push forward to engage; the two levers with black knobs are the steering brakes; the others are transmission and PTO controls.

tinued before the other regulars; the D and the AR were styled.

Finally, the BO Lindeman Crawler conversion was produced between 1939 and 1947. Just as several of the earlier GPOs had been converted by the Lindeman outfit in Yakima, some 2,000 Model BO tractors were also converted to tracks for the steep hillside duty in the western orchards. Some of these were equipped with dozer blades and a hydraulic lift for the blade, also made by Lindeman.

Collecting Comments

Following is a chart of versions of the B by type, serial number, and year built. The star system investment rating is shown for each

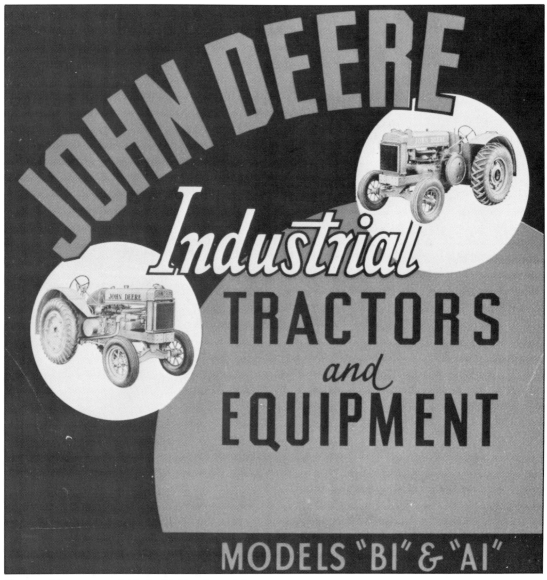

Cover art from a special Industrial tractor catalog featuring the AI and the BI.

type. Note that the serial numbers run consecutively through the year but that the various versions and types are intermingled.

It is necessary to research individual serial numbers at the Deere archives, the Two-Cylinder Club, or other sources to determine a tractor's original configuration. Don't be misled into believing all tractors in the five-star serial number sequences are rare. The four- and five-star tractors are few and far between among ordinary tractors.

The Model B is somewhat more in demand by collectors than are the larger Deeres, because of its smaller size and lower weight. This makes it easier to store and to trailer. Thus, a B will usually fetch a slightly higher price than an equivalent A.

Serial Numbers and Year Models

The following chart is provided as a means of determining a tractor's year model. The model year for the B generally started in August of the preceding calendar year. The number listed is the first serial number of that year. Note that where a major change occurred, serial numbers were skipped so that the new version could begin with an even number for ready recognition.

| | Beginning Serial Number | | |
Year	B-GP	BO and BR	BO Lindeman
1935	1000		
1936	12012	325000	
1937	27389	326655	
1938	46175	328111	
1939	60000	329000	
1940	81600	330633	
1941	96000	332039	
1942	126345	332427	
1943	143420	332780	332901
1944	152862	333156	333110
1945	173179	334219	333666
1946	183673	335641	335361
1947	199744	336746	336441
1948	209295		
1949	237346		
1950	258205		
1951	276557		
1952	299175		

The first numbered tractors arrived in 1952 with the Model 50 to replace the Model B, shown here, and the Model 60 to replace the Model A. The 50 was manufactured through 1956 and was originally rated at 20.62 drawbar hp and 26.32 belt hp, according to the State of Nebraska Test. *Deere & Company*

Model 50

Quoting the writers of *Two-Cylinder*, "It's time for the '50' to be recognized as a real gem in the line of John Deere two-cylinder tractors." The Model 50 is old enough to be interesting but modern enough to be exciting. Because of its newness, parts are in ready supply; because of its ruggedness,

Model 50 Specifications		
Years produced:		1952–1956
First serial number:		5000001
Last serial number:		5033751
Total built:		32,574 (approx.)
Price, new:		$2,100 (1954)
	Drawbar Hp	**PTO/Belt Hp**
Engine		
Gasoline	27.5	31
Tractor fuel	23.2	25.8
LPG	29.2	32.3
General Specifications		
Engine displacement		190ci
Engine bore and stroke		4.69x5.5in
Engine rated rpm		1250
Tires, standard		
Rear		10x38 or 11x38
Front		5.5x16
Length		132.75in
Height to radiator		59.9in
Weight		4,435lb
Transmission		
Speeds forward		6
Reverse		1

collectors find examples in relatively good shape. The main disadvantage to the collector is that the usefulness of Model 50s on the farm has not diminished enough to make them surplus.

The decision by Deere, in 1951, to change from letter designations to numbers was a significant marketing step. This was done to modernize the image of the John Deere tractor—to give it a postwar update. To make the demarcation even more clear, the serial numbering systems were changed to begin with the model number; for example, 5000001 was the first Model 50. Although company records initially contain the N and W front end suffixes, these were not used with the trade.

After serial number 5001101, front end designators were dropped. Since the effort was being made to convince buyers that the new tractors were truly convertible, Deere decided not even to indicate the original configuration on the build records.

This now presents a dilemma for the collector. Informed guesses and extrapolations from earlier records indicate that more than 85 percent of the 32,574 Model 50s built were dual narrow-front and Roll-O-Matic–front gasoline types. This means that all other variations are extremely rare, except that they

This 1953 photo, taken in Blytheville, Arkansas, shows a Model 50 tractor pulling a Hay Baler 116W.

The Model 50 succeeded the B in 1952. *Deere & Company*

are readily convertible. And, since no original-configuration records were kept on most of them, it's perfectly legal as a collector to make your 50 into a version with a rarer front end.

The Model B, which the 50 was replacing in the 1953 model year, had been last revised in 1947, and it had been in inventory for eighteen years. During this time, the horse had, for the most part, been replaced, and now competition was from other brands of tractors.

The new 50 had many improvements to tout when it was introduced in late 1952. The engine was the same in displacement and rated speed, but improvements in carburetion and the cylinder intake passages resulted in about 10 percent more horsepower. Live hydraulics with more power and a live PTO were also now available, along with Deere's version of the three-point hitch. The changing of rear wheel spacing was improved with a rack-and-pinion adjusting mechanism.

Finally, a water pump and a thermostat were added, and for the first time Deere tractors no longer relied on the simple, effective, but old-fashioned thermosyphon cooling system. With this change came a smaller pressurized radiator, using more steel and less copper—which was, because of the Korean War, a critical military material—and employing higher normal operating temperatures. Gone also were the manually operated radiator shutters, replaced with thermostatically controlled shutters.

With the introduction of the 50 and other numbered tractors, the pressed steel frame was replaced with the cast steel frame of the type that was used before 1947. This was done, according to advertisements of the day, to provide increased strength for the variety of front end arrangements while maintaining a more equal front end height with all variations.

Model 50 Variations

Although the all-fuel option was maintained on the 50, the magneto ignition option was dropped in favor of battery ignition. Later, in 1955, an LPG version was added. The Model 50 was available in row-crop versions only, and in dual, dual Roll-O-Matic, single or wide-tread front end arrangements. Otherwise, except for up-swept or down-swept exhaust, no changes or variations were made during the life of the Model 50.

Collecting Comments

Following is a chart of versions of the 50. The star system investment rating is shown

Rating	Model	Years	Serial Numbers	Remarks
★★	50	1952–1956	5000001–5033751	Gasoline engine, dual front and Roll-O-Matic
★★★	50	1952–1956	5000001–5033751	Gasoline engine, wide front
★★★	50	1952–1956	5000001–5033751	Gasoline engine, single front wheel
★★★	50	1952–1956	5000001–5033751	All-fuel engine, dual front and Roll-O-Matic
★★★★	50	1952–1956	5000001–5033751	All-fuel engine, wide front
★★★★	50	1952–1956	5000001–5033751	All-fuel engine, single front wheel
★★★★	50	1955–1956	5021977–5033751	LPG engine, dual front and Roll-O-Matic
★★★★	50	1955–1956	5021977–5033751	LPG engine, wide front
★★★★	50	1955–1956	5021977–5033751	LPG engine, single front wheel

for each type. Note that although the serial numbers run consecutively through the years, the various versions are intermingled randomly in the sequence.

Although the 50s had grown to be more like the early As than the Bs they replaced, they are still a manageable size and weight for most collectors. The 50s are also desirable from a collecting standpoint because relatively few were made, as compared with the number of ubiquitous As and Bs. But because of their convertibility, not as much credit can be given for the rarer front end types.

Serial Numbers and Year Models

The following chart provides a means of determining a tractor's year model. Note that some numbers in the sequence were skipped, or scrapped, as only 32,574 Model 50s were built according to Deere production records, whereas the serial number sequence indicates a total 33,751 possible.

Year	Beginning Serial Number
1952	5000001
1953	5001254
1954	5016041
1955	5021977
1956	5030600

The last Model 50 serial number was 5033751.

Model 520

The severe competition in the tractor business in the mid-fifties kept both engineering and marketing people busy at Deere. The new numbered tractor series had just been completed in 1955 with the introduction of the Model 80, when stirrings began for a complete new line-up. The main driver for the new line was the availability of Deere's version of Draft Control, which was called Custom Powr-Trol.

To go along with the new Custom Powr-Trol came increased power for the 520 over that for the previous Model 50. Although engine displacement stayed the same, the rpm were upped to 1325 from the previous 1250. Cylinder heads and combustion chambers were also improved, resulting in a 25 percent horsepower increase over that of the Model 50.

Operator comfort was also emphasized on the 520, with power steering now being standard equipment. Also available was an optional Float-Ride seat, cushioned by rubber torsion springs that could be adjusted to the operator's weight.

Styling was basically unchanged between the 520 and the 50, except that the new 520, like all the 20 Series tractors, had a two-tone paint job, with the yellow being prominent on panels as well as the wheels.

Rating	Model	Years	Serial Numbers	Remarks
★★	520	1956–1958	5200000–5213189	Gasoline engine, dual front and Roll-O-Matic
★★	520	1956–1958	5200000–5213189	Gasoline engine, wide front
★★★	520	1956–1958	5200000–5213189	Gasoline engine, single front wheel
★★★★	520	1956–1958	5200000–5213189	All-fuel engine, dual front and Roll-O-Matic
★★★★	520	1956–1958	5200000–5213189	All-fuel engine, wide front
★★★★	520	1956–1958	5200000–5213189	All-fuel engine, single front wheel
★★★★	520	1956–1958	5200000–5213189	LPG engine, dual front and Roll-O-Matic
★★★★	520	1956–1958	5200000–5213189	LPG engine, wide front
★★★★	520	1956–1958	5200000–5213189	LPG engine, single front wheel

The Model 520 arrived with the 20 Series in 1956 as a replacement for the Model 50, with an all-new engine design. The new engine featured an improved cylinder head and pistons that provided better combustion chamber turbulence and more horsepower. The 520 was originally rated at 25.63 drawbar hp and 32.38 belt hp, according to the State of Nebraska Test. *Deere & Company*

Model year 1956 was one of many improvements in the John Deere tractor line, led by a 20 percent power increase for all models. Also featured was an improved hydraulic three-point hitch system with true Draft Control. This accurately restored 1956 Model 520 poses for the camera during Two-Cylinder Days at Grand Detour, Illinois.

Collecting Comments

Following is a chart of versions of the 520. The star system investment rating is shown for each type. Note that although the serial numbers run consecutively through the years, the various versions are intermingled.

The 520, like the Model 50 it replaced, is also desirable from a collecting standpoint, because relatively few were made. Also as in the case of the 50, because of their convertibility, not much credit can be given for the rarer front end types.

Serial Numbers and Year Models

The following chart provides a means of determining a tractor's year model:

Year	Beginning Serial Number
1956	5200000
1957	5202982
1958	5209029

The last Model 520 serial number was 5213189.

Model 530

What was left for Marketing and Engineering to do for the little brother tractor after the

Model 520 Specifications

Years produced:		1956–1958
First serial number:		5200000
Last serial number:		5213189
Total built:		13,000 (approx.)
Price, new:		$2,300 (1958)

Engine	Drawbar Hp	PTO/Belt Hp
Gasoline	34.31	38.58
Tractor fuel	24.77	26.61
LPG	34.17	38.09

General Specifications	
Engine displacement	190ci
Engine bore and stroke	4.69x5.5in
Engine rated rpm	1325
Tires, standard	
Rear	12.4x36
Front	5.5x16
Length	132.75in
Height to radiator	59.9in
Weight	4,960lb
Transmission	
Speeds forward	6
Reverse	1

20 Series improvements? Deere had the competition blanketed with sizes and horsepowers, especially with the introduction of the new Model 435, so increasing the power

The Model 530 made its debut with the 30 Series as a replacement for the 20 Series, with an emphasis on more power and operator convenience and comfort. Introduced in 1958, it continued in production into 1961. It was advertised at 34.31 drawbar hp and 38.58 belt hp. *Deere & Company*

Model 530 Specifications

Years produced:		1958–1960
First serial number:		5300000
Last serial number:		5309814
Total built:		9,813 (approx.)
Price, new:		$2,400 (1960)

Engine	Drawbar Hp	PTO/Belt Hp
Gasoline	34.31	38.58
Tractor fuel	24.77	26.61
LPG	34.17	38.09

General Specifications

Engine displacement	190ci
Engine bore and stroke	4.69x5.5in
Engine rated rpm	1325
Tires, standard	
Rear	12.4x36
Front	5.5x16
Length	132.75in
Height to radiator	59.9in
Weight	4,960lb
Transmission	
Speeds forward	6
Reverse	1

or weight of this two-three plow line would be of little use.

Yet, customers had a large choice of tractors from the eight major American wheel-type tractor makers in 1958. Productivity was the competitive key, so the Deere staff launched a program that would include all of its tractors and would be aimed at operator comfort and convenience. Such improvements would thereby allow the operator to work more hours without expending any more personal energy.

Fender handholds and an axle step made mounting the new 530 a much easier task. Once the operator was seated in the improved Float-Ride seat, the new angled shaft

Rating	Model	Years	Serial Numbers	Remarks
★★	530	1958–1960	5300000–5309814	Gasoline engine, dual front and Roll-O-Matic
★★	530	1958–1960	5300000–5309814	Gasoline engine, wide front
★★★	530	1958–1960	5300000–5309814	Gasoline engine, single front wheel
★★★★	530	1958–1960	5300000–5309814	All-fuel engine, dual front and Roll-O-Matic
★★★★	530	1958–1960	5300000–5309814	All-fuel engine, wide front
★★★★	530	1958–1960	5300000–5309814	All-fuel engine, single front wheel
★★★★	530	1958–1960	5300000–5309814	LPG engine, dual front and Roll-O-Matic
★★★★	530	1958–1960	5300000–5309814	LPG engine, wide front
★★★★	530	1958–1960	5300000–5309814	LPG engine, single front wheel

steering wheel was immediately apparent because of the more comfortable and convenient angle. Also, the new flat-topped fenders deflected mud and dust and provided an ideal mounting place for the new four-lamp headlight system—which, of course, encouraged round-the-clock operation.

Also new was an improved lighted instrument panel with all switches and gauges convenient for the operator; the panel even included a cigarette lighter for the first time.

Some technical improvements were made as well. Although the engine specifications stayed the same, materials and construction were changed to make the engine even more durable. Power-adjusted rear wheel spacing was also featured, along with a new oval muffler for quieter operation.

Collecting Comments

Following is a chart of versions of the 530. The star system investment rating is shown for each type. Note that although the serial numbers run consecutively through the years, the various versions are intermingled. No records were kept on the original front end configuration.

Though not at all in the antique category, the 530 is desirable from a collecting standpoint because so few were made. The 530, like the other 30s, represents the culmination of the breed; the finest of the Little Brother tractors; the pinnacle of development. As with the 50 and 520, however, not much credit can be given for the rarer front end types because of the easy convertibility. It is

A pretty Model 530 Wide-Front, owned by Gerald and Ken Funfsinn. This is a 1959 model, the last of the fabled B line.

known that fewer than 420 of the LPG versions were produced, so they rate high regardless of the front end type.

Serial Numbers and Year Models

The following chart provides a means of determining a tractor's year model:

Year	Beginning Serial Number
1958	5300000
1959	5301671
1960	5307749

The last Model 530 serial number was 5309814.

Chapter 8

John Deere Models G, 70, 720, and 730

Big Brother

As the decade of the thirties drew to a close, the progressive farmers—especially those whose lands had not suffered extensively during the drought of the beginning of the decade—had, for the most part, outgrown their horses. Now they were in the market for tractors that would handle larger implements, move them faster, and further multi-

A 1937 G powers a threshing machine. You know the power is adequate when a thresher can be fed from both sides! *Deere & Company*

THE G

INTEGRAL EQUIPMENT

TWO-WAY PLOW.

TWO-, THREE-, AND FOUR-ROW BEDDERS.

TWO-ROW MIDDLEBREAKER.

TWO- OR FOUR-ROW BEDDER-PLANTERS.

TWO-ROW LISTERS.

TWO-ROW COTTON, CORN, AND PEANUT PLANTER. (Available with or without fertilizer or pea attachment.)

TWO - ROW COMBINATION UNIT. (For bedding or furrowing, planting and fertilizing in one operation.)

FOUR-ROW COTTON AND CORN PLANTER.

TWO-ROW CULTIVATORS.

ATTACHMENTS FOR TWO-ROW CULTIVATORS:

TWO-ROW FERTILIZER AT-TACHMENT.

TWO- OR FOUR-ROW BEAN HARVESTER ATTACHMENTS.

VARIABLE-ROW TOOL-BAR ATTACHMENT. (For cultivating beets, beans, and other vegetables.)

TWO-ROW PEANUT PULLER ATTACHMENTS.

TWO - ROW DISK CULTIVA-TORS.

FOUR-ROW CULTIVATORS.

FERTILIZER ATTACHMENT. (For Four-Row Cultivators.)

VARIABLE - ROW CULTIVA-TORS. (For beets, beans, and other vegetables.)

SWEEP RAKES.

GRAIN SHOCK SWEEP.

ONE- AND TWO-ROW PUSH-TYPE CORN PICKERS.

TWO-ROW BEET LIFTER.

TWO- OR FOUR-ROW BEAN HARVESTER.

TWO-ROW PEANUT PULLER.

THE Model "G"—a full 3-plow tractor—rounds out the John Deere general purpose tractor line. It's a powerful tractor for the larger row-crop farms, built with the same type of two-cylinder engine that has made all John Deere tractors famous.

Because of its ability to handle three-row bedders under all conditions, four-row bedders under most conditions, four-row planters, four-row cultivators, and other large-capacity equipment, the Model "G" appeals especially to the large-acreage cotton or corn grower and to the grain farmer who also raises some cotton or corn. The Model "G" develops ample drawbar power to pull three 14-inch plow bottoms under average conditions. On the belt, it operates machines up to and including a 28-inch thresher. And, a power take-off is standard equipment for operating power-driven machines.

In most other respects, the Model "G" is identical with Models "A" and "B," previously described—tractors that have met the most exacting needs of row-crop farmers in all sections of the country. It has all of the advanced John Deere general purpose features, and it can be furnished with a hydraulic power lift and a variety of large-capacity integral working equipment.

The Model G tractor from a 1941 Deere brochure.
Deere & Company

A nice mid-forties Model G takes its place in the line-up at the Antique Engine Show in Franklin Grove, Illinois.

ply the efforts of human power. This is where the big brother series of John Deere tractors came in, beginning in 1938.

Besides, a sense of accomplishment existed among those who were coming out of the Great Depression first. Sales of automobiles with "midsized" names, such as Dodge and Pontiac, were on the upswing, and 1939 saw the first Mercury automobile. Those with relatively secure jobs were flexing their muscles, and the forty-hour week became the US standard.

At the time, too, was a sense of urgency. Political unrest in Europe and Asia put war clouds on the horizon. Americans seemed willing to work harder and smarter to get their country back on its feet.

Thus, the advent of the big John Deere Model G in 1938 was welcomed by large-

A lovely, late, unstyled Model G with Roll-O-Matic front wheels. Roll-O-Matic lets the wheels independently step over obstacles.

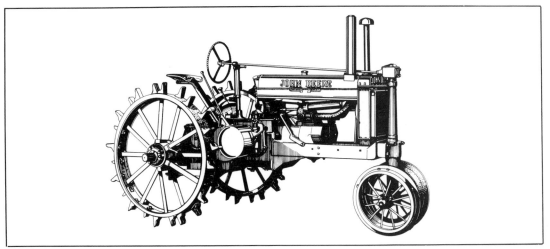

The Model G was the most powerful tractor Deere had constructed up to the time of its introduction in 1938. It was originally rated at 20.7 drawbar hp and 31.44 belt hp, according to the State of Nebraska Test. *Deere & Company*

acreage farmers who needed at least some row-crop capabilities. It was virtually the power equal of the D, which had been their mainstay.

Model G

Production of the G actually began in May of 1937. The model was billed as a full three-plow tractor, meaning it could handle three 16in bottoms in most soils. It had essentially the same power as the D but was about ½ ton lighter. Therefore, more power was available to the drawbar, since not so much was used to overcome the tractor's own weight.

Serial number 11643 means this unstyled Model G was built in 1941; it was one of only 1,508 Gs made that model year.

One of only 4,250 low-radiator Model Gs produced, this 1938 example has cast wheels and a dandy umbrella. Bunky Meese of Freeport, Illinois, owns it. Radiator size was increased on later models to improve cooling.

The owner of this nice late Model G must like the distinctive John Deere sound; note the mufflerless exhaust.

An old Model G. The cast shift quadrant above and to the right of the flywheel is one of the things that differentiate the G from the A, which had no quadrant.

Not long after its introduction, Deere began receiving complaints about the G overheating, especially from farmers in warm climates. Deere finally concluded that its radiator sizing parameters did not extrapolate linearly and that the radiator was indeed too small for the amount of heat being generated.

Accordingly, after serial number 4251, the height of the radiator was increased. Examples produced prior to that serial number are now known as low-radiator Gs. They are extremely rare and of great value to collectors, if equipped with the original radiator. The taller radiator interfered with the overhead steering shaft, so it had a notch in the cast upper tank, which allowed passage of the shaft. Unfortunately, Deere's recall was

Models G and GM Specifications

Years produced:		1938–1953
First serial number:		1000
Last serial number:		64530
Total built:		64,000 (approx.)
Price, new:		$2,600 (1953)

Engine	Drawbar Hp	PTO/Belt Hp
Distillate	34.5	38.1*

General Specifications

Engine displacement	412.5ci
Engine bore and stroke	6.12x7in
Engine rated rpm	975

Wheels and tires, standard

	Wheels	Tires
Rear	51.5x7in	12x38
Front	24x5in	6x16

	Unstyled	GM	Styled
Length	135in	137.5in	137.5in
Height to radiator	61.5in	65.9in	65.9in
Weight	4,400lb	5,624lb	5,624lb

Transmission

Speeds forward	
Early	4
After serial number 13000	6
Reverse	1

*State of Nebraska Test No. 383, 1947.

A rare Model GN undergoing a frame-up restoration in the shop of Lyle Pals.

too effective for today's collectors, and most tractors with pre-4251 serial numbers were converted and the old radiators discarded.

Additional engine modifications were made at serial number 7100 in late 1938, to further improve cooling. These changes can be noted by the much-increased size of the upper water pipe fitting on top of the engine.

The G was one of the last to receive Dreyfuss styling, in 1942. At the same time, it was reidentified as the GM (Modernized) in order to get a price increase past the War Price Board, to cover its upgrade to the new six-speed transmission. After the end of World War II, it again reverted to plain G.

The unstyled G and the GM were available only as dual-front tricycle types. Postwar versions were also available in single-front-wheel, wide-front, and Hi-Crop arrangements.

The Model G is popular today among tractor-pull enthusiasts. The big 412.5ci engine has reportedly been modified to pro-

Rating	Model	Years	Serial Numbers	Remarks
★★★★★	G	1938–1939	1000–4250	Low radiator Unstyled Four-speed
★★★ ★★★	G GM	1939–1941 1941–1946	5500–12192 13000–22112	Unstyled Styled, six-speed Hand start
★★ ★★★ ★★★ ★★★★★	G GW GN GH	1947–1953	23000–64530	Electric start

duce in the neighborhood of 100hp. The all-spur gear transmission and final drive mechanism with its hardened steel gears apparently thrive in this heavy-duty environment. It's no wonder that a large percentage of the Gs produced are still with us.

The G could be distinguished from its A stablemate by the notched radiator and by the sides of the drawbar support, which were parallel on the G, rather than converging at the front, as on the A. Also, unstyled As did not have cast shift guides, as did unstyled Gs, and the broad engine of the G required a bulge in the frame rails. In addition, the post-1947 Gs retained the angle iron frame, rather than using the pressed steel frame, as on the A. Also, the G's stacks were always side-by-side, rather than inline, as on styled As.

Collecting Comments

Following is a chart of versions of the G by type, serial number, and year built. The star system investment rating is shown for each

type. Note that the serial numbers generally run consecutively through the year and that the various versions and types were intermingled. Note also that about forty-five hundred low-radiator Gs were made (see the first item in the chart), but many have had larger radiators subsequently installed.

For the 1939–1941 unstyled G, add a star if the tractor is on original—not cut-down—steel wheels. Five stars go to an unstyled, low-radiator example and to the Hi-Crop. Four stars go to an unstyled, taller-radiator example on original steel wheels. Reduce the rating to three stars if the vehicle is on cut-down steel wheels.

Serial Numbers and Year Models

The following chart provides a means of determining a tractor's year model:

Year	Beginning Serial Number
1938	1000
1939	7734
1940	9321
1941	10489
1942	12069
1943	—
1944	13748
1945	13905
1946	16694
1947	20527
1948	28127
1949	34587
1950	40761
1951	47194
1952	56510
1953	63489

Model 70

Successor to the Model G, the 70 arrived on the scene a year later than the 50 and 60 but with most of the same features. It was originally available with a choice of gasoline, all-fuel, or LPG engines, but later, in 1954, the diesel option was offered.

The 70 was the original "no-neck" of the John Deere row-crop line-up—strong, tough, and born to pull. Power was up a whopping 18 percent over that of the G—even more with engine options other than the all-fuel. This was accomplished with a complete revision of the engine. All types

---

Model 70 Row-Crop Specifications

Years produced:	1953–1956
First serial number:	7000001
Last serial number:	7043757
Total built:	43,757 (approx.; all types)
Price, new:	$3,000 (1956)

Engine	Displacement	Drawbar Hp	PTO/Belt Hp
Gasoline	379.5	44.2	50.4
Tractor fuel	412.5	41	45
LPG	379.5	46.1	52
Diesel	376	45.7	51.5

General Specifications

Engine bore and stroke	
Gasoline and LPG	5.87x7in
All-fuel	6.12x7in
Diesel	6.12x6.4in
Engine rated rpm	975
Diesel engine rated rpm	1125
Tires, standard	
Rear	12-38
Front	6x16
Length	136.4in
Height	65.6in
Weight	
Gas and all-fuel	6,035lb
LPG	6,335lb
Diesel	6,510lb
Transmission	
Speeds forward	6
Reverse	1

except the all-fuel boasted improved air intake passages with the raised eyebrow over
the intake valves, to increase turbulence and
fuel mixing. The nondiesel types had a new
duplex carburetor.

Also new with the Model 70 were live
hydraulics and a live PTO, with a separate
clutch; optional factory-installed power
steering; an adjustable seat backrest; longer
clutch and throttle levers for easier reaching;
and a new rack-and-pinion method of changing rear wheel spacing.

An improved higher-pressure Powr-Trol
had 33 percent more capacity. Dual Touch-
O-Matic hydraulic controls facilitated independent or coordinated raising and lowering
of front or rear implements.

Other features included a 12 volt electrical
system and a rear exhaust option.

The 70 Diesel was Deere's first diesel row-
crop tractor. When tested at the University of
Nebraska, it recorded the lowest fuel consumption for the power output that the
testers had seen, besting all previously

tested row-crop tractors. The 70 used for a
starter a V-4 pony motor of 18.8ci, rather than
the horizontally opposed two-cylinder unit

Model 70S Specifications

Years produced:			1953–1956
First serial number:			7000001
Last serial number:			7043757
Total built:			5,000 (approx.)
Price, new:		\$3,200 (1956); add \$650 for the diesel	

Engine	Displacement	Drawbar Hp	PTO/Belt Hp
Diesel	376	45.7	51.5

General Specifications	
Engine bore and stroke	6.12x6.4in
Engine rated rpm	1125
Tires, standard	
Rear	14-30
Front	6.5x18
Length	129.9in
Height	87.8in
Weight	7,200lb
Transmission	
Speeds forward	6
Reverse	1

The Model 70 was constructed from 1953 to 1956,
arriving one year after Models 50 and 60. It was
originally available with gasoline, all-fuel, or LPG
engines. *Deere & Company*

A Model 70 Hi-Crop LP, one of only twenty-five made. This one is owned by Norman Smith of Carrollton, Illinois.

About all this Model 70 needs is decals.

of the Model R. The pony turned at 5500rpm. Its exhaust heat was routed through parts of the main engine to warm them up.

You could order your 70 in any of five configurations: dual narrow front, wide front, single front wheel, wide-front Hi-Crop, or standard-tread. After 1954, you could choose between four engine options for a total of twenty different combinations.

The 70S (Standard) followed the pattern of the 60NS (New Style), often referred to as the high-seat 60, as it was identical in every way to the row-crop tractor, except for the addition of a straight front axle and different rear fenders.

Collecting Comments

Following is a chart of versions of the 70 by type, serial number, and year built. The star system investment rating is shown for each type. Note that the serial numbers generally

Rating	Model	Years	Serial Numbers	Remarks
★★	70	1953–1956	7000001–7043757	5.9x7in engine Gasoline
★★★	70W			
★★★	70N			
★★★★★★	70H			
★★★★	70S			
★★★	70	1953–1956	7000001–7043757	6.2x7in engine All-fuel
★★★★	70W			
★★★★	70N			
★★★★★★	70H			
★★★★★	70S			
★★	70	1953–1956	7000001–7043757	5.9x7in engine LPG
★★★	70W			
★★★★	70N			
★★★★	70H			
★★★★★	70S			
★★	70D	1953–1956	7000001–7043757	6.2x6.4in engine Diesel
★★★	70DW			
★★★★	70DN			
★★★★★★	70DH			
★★★★	70DS			

A four-spoke steering wheel, as on this Model 70 Wide Front, indicates a tractor without power steering.

The Model 720 was part of the 20 Series that replaced the Model 70 in 1956 and continued to be offered through 1958. It was rated at 40.63 drawbar hp and 50.67 belt hp, according to the State of Nebraska Test. *Deere & Company*

run consecutively through the year but that the various versions and types were sometimes intermingled.

Serial Numbers and Year Models

The following chart provides a means of determining a tractor's year model:

Year	Beginning Serial Number
1953	7000001
1954	7005692
1955	7017501
1956	7034950

Model 720

After a short reign as king of the row-crops, the 70 was replaced by the 720. The new 720 exhibited improvements in virtually every area.

It's hard to consider the Model 720 Diesel in the context of antiques, since it's capable of taking its place with the best of the new tractors. The plaque on the front proclaims the owner is an area coordinator for the Two-Cylinder Club.

With the Custom Powr-Trol, a new position-responsive rock shaft enabled the operator to preset working depth. The operator could raise the implement for a turn at the end of the row and then drop it to the same working depth as before. Also featured was Load-and-Depth Control, Deere's answer to Harry Ferguson's Draft Control. This feature automatically applied raise-pressure to lift the implement when tough soil conditions were encountered, thereby not only lessening the draft load, but also pulling down on the back wheels to improve traction. Once the hard spot was passed, the system automatically returned the implement to its original depth.

Except for the diesel, the engines were all new. Displacement was decreased, but rated rpm were increased from 975 to 1125. This, plus improved cylinder heads and pistons, increased power and reduced fuel consumption.

To increase the productivity of the tractor, the productivity of the operator must also be improved. Therefore, on the 720—as on the other models in the 20 Series—operator comfort and convenience features were added. A new "stand-at-will," more roomy platform was added; the instruments were easier to read; the controls fell more naturally to hand; and the new Float-Ride seat, supported on an adjustable rubber torsion spring and a hydraulic shock absorber, was standard.

Collecting Comments

Following is a chart of versions of the 720 by type, serial number, and year built. The star system investment rating is shown for each type. Note that the serial numbers run consecutively through the year but that the various versions and types are intermingled.

Serial Numbers and Year Models

The following chart provides a means of determining a tractor's year model:

Year	Beginning Serial Number
1956	7200000
1957	7203420
1958	7217368

Model 720 Row-Crop Specifications

Years produced:	1956–1958
First serial number:	7200000
Last serial number:	7229002
Total built:	29,001 (approx.; all types)
Price, new:	$3,700 (1958); add $650 for the diesel

Engine	Displacement	Drawbar Hp	PTO/Belt Hp
Gasoline	360.5	53	59.1
Tractor fuel	360.5	41.3	45.3
LPG	360.5	54.2	59.6
Diesel	376	53.7	58.8

General Specifications

Engine bore and stroke	
Gas, LPG, and all-fuel	6x6.4in
Diesel	6.12x6.4in
Engine rated rpm	1125
Tires, standard	
Rear	12-38
Front	6x16
Length	135.3in
Height	88.3in
Weight	
Gas and all fuel	6,790lb
LPG	7,100lb
Diesel	7,390lb
Transmission	
Speeds forward	6
Reverse	1

Model 720S Specifications

Years produced:	1956–1958
First serial number:	7200000
Last serial number:	7229002
Total built:	3,000 (approx.)
Price, new:	$3,800 (1958); add $650 for the diesel

Engine	Displacement	Drawbar Hp	PTO/Belt Hp
Gasoline	360.5	53	59.1
Tractor fuel	360.5	41.3	45.3
LPG	360.5	54.2	59.6
Diesel	376	53.7	58.8

General Specifications

Engine bore and stroke	
Gas, LPG, and all-fuel	6x6.4in
Diesel	6.12x6.4in
Engine rated rpm	1125
Tires, standard	
Rear	14-30
Front	6.5x18
Length	130.3in
Height	87.1in
Weight	
Gas and all fuel	7,380lb
LPG	7,690lb
Diesel	7,790lb
Transmission	
Speeds forward	6
Reverse	1

Rating	Model	Years	Serial Numbers	Remarks
★★	720	1956–1958	7200000–7229002	6x6.4in engine Gasoline
★★	720W			
★★★	720N			
★★★★	720H			
★★★★★	720S			
★★★	720	1956–1958	7200000–7229002	6x6.4in engine All-fuel
★★★★	720W			
★★★★	720N			
★★★★★★	720H			
★★★★★★	720S			
★★	720	1956–1958	7200000–7229002	6x6.4in engine LPG
★★★	720W			
★★★★	720N			
★★★★★	720H			
★★★★	720S			
★★	720D	1956–1958	7200000–7229002	6.2x6.4in engine Diesel
★★	720DW			
★★★★	720DN			
★★★★★	720DH			
★★★★	720DS			

Model 730

The culmination of the big brother line, the 730 was the ultimate two-cylinder row-crop tractor. It was so capable and modern that despite being well over thirty years old, most examples are still in service and not considered by their owners to be collectible antiques. The only deficiency that might be

A 730 with an 810 plow is shown at the Deere acreage in Moline in 1954. *Deere & Company*

claimed for the 730 against a new tractor costing as much as a small house is that the 730 does not have a multispeed shuttle transmission. As is, the 730's six-speed unit provides enough flexibility for most jobs. An Indiana corn and bean grower who has a plethora of tractors old and new, both John Deere and others—and, by the way, a Ph.D. in engineering—says he'd rather spend a day on his 730 than the newer types, because you can get as much work done for the buck and it's so much more pleasant for the ears.

After the broad range of improvements incorporated into the 720 just two years earlier, you would think not much would be left for a new model. Competition in the tractor business in the late fifties was so intense, however, that no room was available for laurel resting. The 238hp Steiger was born in 1957, indicating the trend of the future.

The Model 730 made its debut with the 30 Series as a replacement for the 20 Series, with an emphasis on more power and operator convenience and comfort. Introduced in 1958, it continued in production into 1961. It was advertised at 53.05 drawbar hp and 59.12 belt hp. *Deere & Company*

A 730 Standard Diesel pulls a pair of DR drills. *Deere & Company*

Case, Minneapolis-Moline, and Oliver also introduced new, capable diesels in 1957. New automatic transmissions were coming in, such as the Case-O-Matic and Ford's Select-O-Speed, as well as torque-amplifier step-down shifters on several competing brands, and the Oliver 995 had a torque converter.

For the 30 Series, Deere concentrated on styling, safety, and comfort. New standard equipment flat-top fenders, with handholds, protected the operator from mud and dust and from accidental contact with the tires. Besides the handholds, a convenient step in front of the axle made mounting and dismounting safer and easier. The fenders also incorporated a new lighting system for improved night work.

A new angled instrument panel featured instruments clustered around the steering

A big Model 730 Diesel. The three-spoke steering wheel indicates power steering, which was standard by then. The flat-top fenders with handholds and the four-light system were also hallmarks of the 30 Series.

Model 730 Row-Crop Specifications

Years produced:			1958–1960
First serial number:			7300000
Last serial number:			7330358
Total built:			30,357 (approx.; all types)
Price, new:			$3,700 (1960)

Engine	Displacement	Drawbar Hp	PTO/Belt Hp
Gasoline	360.5	53	59.1
Tractor fuel	360.5	41.3	45.3
LPG	360.5	54.2	59.6
Diesel	376	53.7	58.8

General Specifications

Engine bore and stroke	
Gas, LPG, and all-fuel	6x6.4in
Diesel	6.12x6.4in
Engine rated rpm	1125
Tires, standard	
Rear	12-38
Front	6x16
Length	135.3in
Height	88.3in
Weight	
Gas and all-fuel	6,790lb
LPG	7,100lb
Diesel	7,390lb
Transmission	
Speeds forward	6
Reverse	1

Model 730S Specifications

Years produced:			1958–1960
First serial number:			7300000
Last serial number:			7330358
Total built:			3,000 (approx.)
Price, new:			$3,900 (1960); add $700 for the diesel

Engine	Displacement	Drawbar Hp	PTO/Belt Hp
Gasoline	360.5	53	59.1
Tractor fuel	360.5	41.3	45.3
LPG	360.5	54.2	59.6
Diesel	376	53.7	58.8

General Specifications

Engine bore and stroke	
Gas, LPG, and all-fuel	6x6.4in
Diesel	6.12x6.4in
Engine rated rpm	1125
Tires, standard	
Rear	14-30
Front	6.5x18
Length	130.3in
Height	87.1in
Weight	
Gas and all-fuel	7,380lb
LPG	7,690lb
Diesel	7,790lb
Transmission	
Speeds forward	6
Reverse	1

Rating	Model	Years	Serial Numbers	Remarks
★★	730	1958–1961	7300000–7330358	6x6.4in engine Gasoline
★★	730W			
★★★	730N			
★★★★★★	730H			
★★★★	730S			
★★★★	730	1958–1961	7300000–7330358	6x6.4in engine All-fuel
★★★★	730W			
★★★★	730N			
★★★★★★	730H			
★★★★★	730S			
★★★	730	1958–1961	7300000–7330358	6x6.4in engine LPG
★★★★	730W			
★★★★	730N			
★★★★★★	730H			
★★★★★	730S			
★★	730D	1958–1961	7300000–7330358	6.2x6.4in engine Diesel
★★	730DW			
★★★	730DN			
★★★★★	730DH			
★★★★	730DS			

column, which now projected upward at a more convenient angle.

Finally, a 24 volt electric starting option was available in place of the V-4 pony motor.

Collecting Comments

Following is a chart of versions of the 730 by type, serial number, and year built. The star system investment rating is shown for each type. Note that the serial numbers run consecutively through the year but that the various versions and types are intermingled. Note also that a run of production was accomplished in 1961 for export. In addition, 730s were built in Argentina throughout the sixties. Any post-1960 tractors found in North America—serial numbers 7328801 and higher—automatically rate five stars.

Serial Numbers and Year Models

The following chart provides a means of determining a tractor's year model:

Year	Beginning Serial Number
1958	7300000
1959	7303761
1960	7322075
1961	7328801

Serial numbers 7328801 to 7330358 in 1961 were built for export.

Chapter 9

John Deere Models H, M, 40, 320, 420, 330, 430, 435, and 440

Twin Brother

From the twenties to the late forties, marketing people and engineers at Deere saw their chief competition not so much from the myriad other tractor makers as from the lowly horse. A large percentage of farmers had two or three teams, and many indeed had only one. It was the goal of the Deere team, from the inception of the GP in 1928, to

The Model H was a small tractor at a price a small farmer could afford, designed to render the draft horse obsolete. It was constructed from 1939 to 1947. It was rated at 9.68 drawbar hp and 12.97 belt hp, according to the State of Nebraska Test. *Deere & Company*

make a tractor that not only appealed to this large, low-end market, but could be seen by small farmers as a quick return on their investment.

Thus, the B was introduced, only to grow to power that rivaled that initially produced by the larger A. In the mid-thirties, Deere developed the L utility series and almost simultaneously the H, with slightly more power but built on the general-purpose arrangement. These were both replaced by the M in the early forties.

This series is nicknamed the twin brother, as the models were all aimed at the market of the twin-horse team. Also, the H was the power twin of the initial Model B. Of course, as is always the case with the Deere tractor lines, power grew with time to where it was doubled in the B, and the 430, successor to the H, actually surpassed the B. By then, however, the competition with the horse had been won.

Model H

"To meet the demands of small-acreage farmers everywhere for a tractor that will handle all power jobs at rock-bottom cost, and meet the demands of the large-acreage farmers who have always wanted and needed economical auxiliary power to handle lighter farm jobs, John Deere offers the new one-two plow Model 'H.'" Thus reads the 1939 sales brochure introducing the new Model H.

The goals undertaken with the design of the H were to do the following:

Some of the unique characteristics of the Model H, Deere's smallest row-crop, are shown in this view: the brakes operating on the axle shafts, rather than on bull gear shafts, as on the other Deeres; the camshaft belt pulley; the small gearshift quadrant; and the hydraulic pump and control, beneath the steering wheel.

• Lower the purchase price through simplified design, improved materials, and reduced parts count.

• Lower the operating cost through balancing of the engine power with the anticipated job, the use of low-cost distillate fuels, and reduced power losses as a result of lightweight construction and the use of large-diameter rubber tires.

• Improve adaptability through adjustable wheel spacing, a three-speed transmission, and a foot-throttle governor override allowing faster road travel.

These design concepts were tested beginning in early 1938 with a series of experimental tractors designated OX138 to OX143. Some of these were unstyled, and some were much the same in appearance as the Models A and B. Apparently, all were scrapped after the introduction of the H in 1939. In fact, only one

or two of the first 100 production Hs are now accounted for, so these too may have been scrapped or rebuilt and given later numbers.

The Model H was unique among the GP tractors in that power was taken off the camshaft rather than the crankshaft. This was done for a number of reasons, all relating to the H engine's 1400rpm rating and ability to be operated—with the governor override—at up to 1800rpm. By taking the power out through the camshaft, a 2:1 reduction was accomplished and the speed was cut in half before coming out of the engine. This meant a simpler transmission and elimination of the bull gears normally used to drive the rear axles. Also, at 1400rpm, the belt pulley would have been too small to provide the desired maximum belt speed of approximately 3,200 feet per minute (fpm). By cutting the speed in half, the H used an oversized belt pulley and

A rare Model HN. The oblong hole ahead of the John Deere decal is the screened air intake used on the H, rather than the above-hood pipe used on the other row-crops.

Rating	Model	Years	Serial Numbers	Remarks
★★	H	1939–1947	1000–61116	3.6x5in engine
★★★★	HN			Distillate
★★★★★	HWH	1941–1942	28493–42842	3.6x5in engine
★★★★★	HNH		30172–42726	Distillate

still only provided a belt speed of 2,245fpm. Interestingly, because of the camshaft mesh, the belt pulley operated in the opposite direction from that of the conventional belt pulley.

Because of the low output speed of the H engine, the usual bull gears at each axle were not required. Elimination of the bull gears meant that the wheel brakes had to be directly on the axle shafts, rather than on the bull gear shafts, as was the usual Deere configuration. Internally expanding shoe-type brakes were provided.

Four versions of the H were produced:
Model H. The H was a dual narrow-front row-crop.
Model HN. The HN was the same as the H but with a single front wheel. It was designed for the California vegetable grower, and approximately 1,100 were built.
Model HWH. The HWH was the same as the H but with 8-38 rear tires and an adjustable wide front axle to provide a minimum crop clearance of 21.4in. Only about 125 were built.
Model HNH. The HNH was the same as the HWH but with a single front wheel. Very few of the thirty-seven HNHs are still known to exist.

Collecting Comments

Following is a chart of versions of the H by type, serial number, and year built. The star system investment rating is shown for each type. Note that the serial numbers run consecutively through the year, but that the Hi-Crop versions are intermingled in the 1941–1942 production.

Serial Numbers and Year Models

The following chart provides a means of determining a tractor's year model:

Model H Specifications

Years produced:		1939–1947
First serial number:		1000
Last serial number:		61116
Total built:		60,000 (approx.)
Price, new:		$650 (1940)

	Drawbar	PTO/Belt
Engine	Hp	Hp
Distillate	12.5	14.8

General Specifications	
Engine displacement	99.7ci
Engine bore and stroke	3.56x5in
Engine rated rpm	1400
Tires, standard	
Rear	8x32
Front	4x15
Length	111.3in
Height to top of radiator	52in
Weight	3,035lb
Transmission	
Speeds forward	3
Reverse	1

A nearly perfect Model H on display in the lobby at Deere World Headquarters.

The Model M arrived following World War II and was designed as a general-purpose utility tractor. It was constructed from 1947 to 1952. In 1947, it was rated at 14.39 drawbar hp and 18.21 belt hp, according to the State of Nebraska Test. *Deere & Company*

The Model MT was a tricycle version of the Model M and was constructed from 1949 to 1952. In 1949, it was rated at 14.08 drawbar hp and 18.33 belt hp, according to the State of Nebraska Test. *Deere & Company*

Year	Beginning Serial Number
1939	1000
1940	10780
1941	23654
1942	40995
1943	44755
1944	47796
1945	48392
1946	55956
1947	60107

Model M

By the end of World War II, it was becoming fairly obvious to the management of Deere, and to that of other tractor manufacturers, that the Ford-Ferguson was winning the battle for the hearts and minds of the farmer with less than 100 acres. The Ford-Ferguson, with its hydraulic three-point hitch for mounted implements, was selling for around the same money as the H. The squat little Ford, however, could plow twelve acres while an H did seven.

For the years 1939 to 1947, Deere averaged about 25,000 tractors a year for the small-farm market. This number included Models B, L, LA, and H. In the same time, Ford-Ferguson sold an average 42,000 a year of its only model. The configuration of this tractor was a combination wide-front, standard-tread, and orchard model. In it, the Deere and other marketing organizations saw the beginning of the trend away from the tricycle front end.

To counter Ford's inroad into the small-farm marketplace, the John Deere Model M was born, replacing the L, LA, and H. The M was billed as a general-purpose utility tractor. It came equipped with a gasoline-only, vertical, relatively high speed 1650rpm two-cylinder engine—a departure from the customary horizontal engine. It also had the Touch-O-Matic rear implement hydraulic lift.

The M's configuration did not satisfy all of Deere's customers, however, so in traditional Deere fashion, the MT was added to the line of 1949. The MT was essentially the same tractor but could be equipped with an adjustable wide front, dual tricycle front, or single front wheel. Dual Touch-O-Matic was an added option, allowing independent control of right and left side implements.

The one place Deere was free from the Ford's competition was in the area of small crawlers. The success of the Lindeman conversions of the Model BO, led, in 1946, to the

Deere purchase of the Lindeman factory in Yakima, and the rights for the crawler tracks. To an M, sans wheels, shipped to Yakima, tracks and controls were added. Thus was born the MC—the first Deere-designed crawler.

Also in 1949, the Model MI (Industrial) was added to the line. Production of this number reached 1,032 units and continued into 1955.

Although this series of unique and useful little tractors was extremely durable, productive, and popular, Ford still sold five times as many 8Ns between 1947 and 1952 as Deere sold all variations of the M.

Collecting Comments

Following is a chart of versions of the M by type, serial number, and year built. The star

An MC in 1950 in McMinnville, Oregon. *Deere & Company*

Model M Specifications		
Years produced:		1947–1952
First serial number:		10001
Last serial number:		50580
Total built:		40,580 (approx.)
Price, new:		$1,075 (1952)
Engine	**Drawbar Hp**	**PTO/Belt Hp**
Gasoline	18.2	20.5
General Specifications		
Engine displacement		100.5ci
Engine bore and stroke		4x4in
Engine rated rpm		1650
Tires, standard		
Rear		8-24
Front		4x15
Length		110in
Height to top of radiator		56in
Weight		2,550lb
Transmission		
Speeds forward		4
Reverse		1

Model MT Specifications		
Years produced:		1949–1952
First serial number:		10001
Last serial number:		35845
Total built:		25,845 (approx.)
Price, new:		$1,200 (1952)
Engine	**Drawbar Hp**	**PTO/Belt Hp**
Gasoline	18.8	21.6
General Specifications		
Engine displacement		100.5ci
Engine bore and stroke		4x4in
Engine rated rpm		1650
Tires, standard		
Rear		9-34
Front		5x15
Length		125.4in
Height to top of radiator		58in
Weight		2,900lb
Transmission		
Speeds forward		4
Reverse		1

The Model MT, introduced in 1949, could be obtained with a dual Roll-O-Matic front, as shown; a single front wheel; or an adjustable wide front axle.

system investment rating is shown for each type. Note that the serial numbers run consecutively through the year but that each sequence begins with serial number 10001.

Serial Numbers and Year Models

The following chart provides a means of determining a tractor's year model:

Year	Beginning Serial Number		
	M	MT	MC
1947	10001		
1948	13743		
1949	25604	10001	10001
1950	35659	18544	11630
1951	43525	26203	13630
1952	50580	35845	16309

Model MC Specifications

Years produced:		1949–1952
First serial number:		10001
Last serial number:		20509
Total built:		10,509 (approx.)
Price, new:		$2,100 (1952)

Engine	Drawbar Hp	PTO/Belt Hp
Gasoline	18.3	22.2

General Specifications

Engine displacement	100.5ci
Engine bore and stroke	4x4in
Engine rated rpm	1650
Length	102in
Height to top of radiator	50.5in
Weight	4,000lb
Transmission	
Speeds forward	4
Reverse	1

The Woods mower drive mechanism dominates this view of a 1950 Model M.

The vertical-engine Model MT with dual narrow front, modern and capable 20hp tractor, was Deere's answer to the Ford 8N. This one has the grille of a Model 40, however.

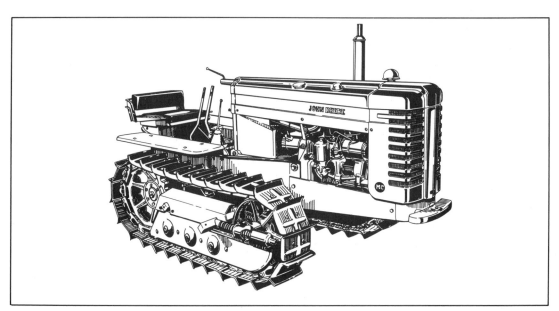

Although the Model BO was Deere's first crawler, the track construction was done by Lindeman. The Model MC was the first crawler tractor built completely by Deere, in production from 1949 to 1952. *Deere & Company*

Rating	Model	Years	Serial Numbers	Remarks
★★	M	1947–1952	10001–50580	4x4in vertical gasoline engine
★★★	MT	1949–1952	10001–35845	Dual narrow front
★★★	MT-W			Wide front
★★★★	MT-N			Single front
★★★★★	MC	1949–1952	10001–20509	Crawler
★★★★	MI	1949–1955	10001–11032	Industrial

This 1949 Model M was given to the owner of the spread's wife by her grandfather. That suggests one way to avoid conflict with your tractor-collecting hobby: get your mate involved. The mechanisms on the side are for a front bucket.

Model 40 Specifications		
Years produced:		1953–1956
First serial number:		60001
Last serial number:		77906
Total built:		33,000 (approx.)
Price, new:		$1,500 (1954)
	Drawbar	**PTO/Belt**
Engine	**Hp**	**Hp**
Gasoline	22.4	24.9
Tractor fuel	19	20.9
General Specifications		
Engine displacement		100.5ci
Engine bore and stroke		4x4in
Engine rated rpm		1850
Tires, standard	40S	40T
Rear	9-24	9-34
Front	5x15	5x15
Length	114.3in	130.6in
Height to radiator	56in	59in
Weight	2,750lb	3,000lb
Transmission		
Speeds forward		4
Reverse		1

Model 40

In 1953, the numbered series of John Deere tractors was introduced, and the 40S (Standard), the 40T (Tricycle), and the 40C (Crawler) replaced the M, MT, and MC on the Dubuque, Iowa, assembly line. The new tractors shared styling and technical features with their Waterloo relatives.

Nameplate designations for the different versions of the Model 40 were as follows:

C   Crawler
S   Standard
H   Hi-Crop
T   Tricycle (all tricycle styles were labeled T)
W   Two-Row Utility
V   Special
U   Utility

The 40 had the new deep-fluted radiator grille, and it had larger fuel tanks than its M

The Model 40 line was introduced in 1953 as a replacement for the M, MT, and MC line. Shown is the 40 Tricycle version, constructed through 1955.

In 1953, the 40 Tricycle was rated at 17.16 drawbar hp and 21.45 belt hp, according to the State of Nebraska Test. *Deere & Company*

predecessors. An improved battery compartment made battery service easier, and the platform boasted easier mounting and dismounting and a more comfortable seat. A true three-point hitch was added, along with live hydraulics. The four-speed transmission, self-energizing brakes, adjustable wheel tread, and PTO of the M Series were retained on the 40 Series.

The 40 Series also had about 15 percent more power than the M. Engine displacement stayed the same, but rated rpm were raised to 1850. This, plus internal improvements, led to the horsepower boost. Along with this improved gasoline engine, the all-fuel engine was introduced, except for the 40C.

The 40C had a much-improved track running gear, with a choice of either four or five rollers. The MC system, with only three rollers, left something to be desired in durability, traction, and stability, especially when using the front bulldozer blade. Most 40Cs came equipped with a radiator shield made of heavy perforated sheet metal. Hydraulics to operate the bulldozer blade was an option.

A Model 40T, with a spring-tooth harrow. *Deere & Company*

Rating	Model	Years	Serial Numbers	Remarks
★★	40S	1953–1955	60001–71814	Standard
★★	40U	1953–1955	60001–71689	Low adjustable
★★★★	40W	1955	60001–63140	Wide low
★★★★★	40V	1955	60001–60329	26in clearance
★★★★★★	40H	1954–1955	60001–60060	32in clearance
★★	40T-W	1953–1956	60001–75531	Wide front
★★★	40T-RC			Dual narrow front
★★★★	40T-N			Single front wheel
★★	40C	1953–1955	60001–77906	4 rollers
★★★				5 rollers

A Model 40S tractor, with a Panbreaker implement.
Deere & Company

A three-point hitch was not available. Most 40Cs were built in Dubuque, since the Yakima plant closed in 1954.

Model 40 Variations

The 40U, also introduced in 1953, was lower than the S. The 40W, brought out in 1955, was low and had provisions for extra-wide wheel adjustments. In 1954 and 1955, two other variations of the 40 appeared: the 40H, with 32in of clearance, and the 40V, with 26in of clearance.

Collecting Comments

Following is a chart of versions of the 40 by type, serial number, and year built. The star system investment rating is shown for each type. All versions began with the same serial

Model 40C Specifications		
Years produced:		1953–1956
First serial number:		60001
Last serial number:		77906
Total built:		17,000 (approx.)
Price, new:		$2,500 (1956)
	Drawbar	**PTO/Belt**
Engine	**Hp**	**Hp**
Gasoline	20.1	24.9
General Specifications		
Engine displacement		100.5ci
Engine bore and stroke		4x4in
Engine rated rpm		1850
Length		102.6in
Height to top of radiator		60in
Weight		4,000lb
Transmission		
Speeds forward		4
Reverse		1

An early Dubuque-built Model 40 Tricycle. The live-hydraulics three-point hitch was improved over the Model M system. This one is owned by Francis Peters.

127

A Model 40W. *Deere & Company*

number—60001—and then followed their own sequences. All used the vertical 4x4in engine, and all except the 40C could have the

The Model 320 was designed as part of the 20 Series to be a small utility tractor. It was introduced in 1956 with the series and continued to be offered until 1958. It was rated as a one- or two-plow tractor. *Deere & Company*

all-fuel, instead of gasoline, option. Add another star to the rating, unless it is already five stars, for the all-fuel tractors.

Serial Numbers and Year Models

The following chart provides a means of determining a tractor's year model:

Year	40V	40S	40U	40H	40T	40W	40C
		Beginning Serial Number					
1953		60001	60001		60001		60001
1954		67359	60202	60001	72167		63358
1955	60001	69474	63140	60060	75531	60001	66894

Model 320

Designed especially for the vegetable grower and small farmer, the 320 was again an attempt to reach the smallest user. It came in two versions: the 320S (Standard) and the 320U (Utility). The 320S boasted a crop clearance of 21in, which appealed to such farmers as berry, peanut, vegetable, and tobacco growers. The 320U—with its shortened front spindles and geared offset rear axles, rather than the direct-drive axles of the S— was about 5in lower. It appealed to orchard-

Model 320 Specifications

	Years produced:		1956–1958
	First serial number:		320001
	Last serial number:		325518
	Total built:		3,083 (approx.)
	Price, new:		$1,900 (1958)

Engine	Drawbar Hp	PTO/Belt Hp
Gasoline	22.4	24.9

General Specifications

Engine displacement		100.5ci
Engine bore and stroke		4x4in
Engine rated rpm		1850
Tires, standard		
Rear		9-24
Front		5x15

	320S	320U
Length	115.7in	119.3in
Height to radiator	56in	50in
Weight		2,750lb
Transmission		
Speeds forward		4
Reverse		1

An extremely rare 320 Southern Special. This is essentially a factory-modified 320 with the front axle and rear wheels of a 420 Special. *Reed Gerber*

Using the same engine as the earlier M Series, the Model 320 was a 22hp tractor.

Rating	Model	Years	Serial Numbers	Remarks
★★★★	320	1956	320001–3202566	4x4in gasoline engine
★★★★	320S	1956–1958	325001–325518	
★★★★	320U			

ists, mowers, and operators who used tractors inside buildings or in areas of limited clearance.

The engine of the 320 was the same 4x4in unit of the Model 40 and was therefore not tested at the University of Nebraska.

The 320 retained the productivity features of the big tractors, including disk brakes, push-button starting, the new Float-Ride seat that was adjustable for the operator's weight, Touch-O-Matic live hydraulics, and the load-compensating three-point hitch called Load-and-Depth Control.

As with the others in the 20 Series, the 320 could be distinguished by horizontal and vertical bands of yellow paint on the hood.

The main advantage offered by the 320 was low cost, both in purchase price and in operation. With fewer than 3,100 built, collectors are today rapidly eliminating the low-purchase-price advantage.

Collecting Comments

Following is a chart of versions of the 320 by type, serial number, and year built. The star system investment rating is shown for each type. Note that the serial numbers run consecutively through the year but that the various versions and types are intermingled. The first 2,566 units produced carried only the 320 designation; thereafter, this configuration was given the designation 320S and another lower version was given the designation 320U. Production of the S and U versions began a new sequence with serial number 325001.

Serial Numbers and Year Models

The following chart provides a means of determining a tractor's year model:

Year	Beginning Serial Number
1956	320001
1957	321220
1958	325127

Model 420

The Model 420, introduced in 1956, was much the same as the 40 it replaced but with some important improvements. These included a 20 percent power increase accomplished mainly by increasing the bore by 0.25in; a live PTO; a pressurized radiator with a water pump; dual Touch-O-Matic for the Standard and a hydraulic three-point hitch for the Crawler; and in 1957, the LPG option.

Eight configurations were included, as follows:

420S (Standard) with an adjustable wide front and 22in of clearance

Model 420 Specifications			
Years produced:			1956–1958
First serial number:			80001
Last serial number:			136868
Total built:		55,000 (approx.; all types)	
Price, new:			$2,300 (1958)
	Drawbar Hp		**PTO/Belt Hp**
Engine			
Gasoline	27.1		29.2
Tractor fuel	21.9		23.5
LPG	28		30
General Specifications			
Engine displacement			113.5ci
Engine bore and stroke			4.25x4in
Engine rated rpm			1850
Tires, standard	420S	420T	420W
Rear	9-24	9-24	10-24
Front, all types			5x15
Length	114.8in	114.8in	119.3in
Height to radiator	56in	56in	56in
Weight	2,750lb	3,000lb	3,250lb
Transmission			
Speeds forward			
Standard			4
Optional			5
Reverse			1

The Model 420 was offered in a series of tractors including a Standard, a dual-wheel tricycle front end, a single-wheel front end, a wide-axle front end, a Hi-Crop, and a Special with 27in clearance over the rows and a variety of wheel spacings. Introduced in 1956 with the 20 Series, it continued to be offered until 1958. *Deere & Company*

A Model 420 Wide Front. Introduced in 1956, the 420 offered a number of new optional features, such as a live PTO and a five-speed gearbox.

420U (Utility) with an adjustable wide front and 17in of clearance
420W (Two-Row Utility) with a low wide front and adjustable width
420H (Hi-Crop) with a wide front and 32in of clearance
420V (Special)

420T (Row-Crop) with a dual narrow front
420I (Special Utility)
420C (Crawler) with either four or five rollers

Especially in the 420T configuration, this tractor looked like its larger family relatives. And in the gasoline engine version, it sur-

A crawler tractor, Model 420C, in 1957, with a Series 400 toolbar. *Deere & Company*

passed the venerable B in power and was essentially the equal of the Model 50. It was considerably lighter than the late-styled B and the 50 but was about the equal of the early-styled Bs.

The 420C was again beefed up to handle the types of chores it was being assigned: chores in construction and forestry that imposed much higher loads than did those of routine farming. Like the 40C, it was available in either the four- or five-roller track configurations; with the later, longer, configuration, maneuverability was somewhat sacrificed for increased flotation and stability. New for the 420C was the return of the all-fuel engine option.

The 420s produced early in the production run were all green until the 20 series tractors were introduced. Thereafter, they received the distinguishing horizontal and vertical bands of yellow paint on the hood.

Collecting Comments

Following is a chart of versions of the 420 by type, serial number, and year built. The star system investment rating is shown for each type. Note that all versions are intermixed in the serial number sequence. All types used the 4.25x4in engine; gasoline, all-fuel, and LPG variations were made. Add a star for all-fuel and LPG versions.

Model 420C Specifications

Years produced:		1956–1958
First serial number:		80001
Last serial number:		136868
Total built:		20,000 (approx.)
Price, new:		$3,300 (1958)

Engine	Drawbar Hp	PTO/Belt Hp
Gasoline	24.1	29.7
Tractor fuel	20	24
LPG	24	30

General Specifications

Engine displacement	113.5ci
Engine bore and stroke	4.25x4in
Engine rated rpm	1850
Length	102in
Height to top of radiator	52in
Weight	4,150lb
Transmission	
Speeds forward	
Standard	4
Optional	5
Reverse	1

Serial Numbers and Year Models

The following chart provides a means of determining a tractor's year model:

Year	Beginning Serial Number
1956	80001
1957	107813
1958	127782

Rating	Model	Years	Serial Numbers	Remarks
★★	420S	1956–1958	80001–136866	Standard nonadjustable front
★★★	420U			Low adjustable front
★★★	420W			2-row low wide utility
★★★★★	420H			Hi-Crop, 32in clearance
★★★★★	420V			Special, 26in clearance
★★★★	420I			
★★★	420T RC	1956–1958	80001–136866	Dual narrow front
★★★	420T W			Adjustable wide front
★★★	420T N			Single front wheel
★★★	420C	1956–1958	80001–136866	4-roller crawler
★★★★	420C			5-roller crawler
				Gas and all-fuel engines only

The Model 330 made its debut with the 30 Series as a replacement for the 20 Series, with an emphasis on more power and operator convenience and comfort. Introduced in 1958, it continued in production into 1961. It had power to pull two 12in bottom plows and was advertised at 21.5 belt hp. *Deere & Company*

Model 330

The 330 was essentially the same tractor as the 320 it succeeded in 1958, with the same two variations: the 330S (Standard) and the 330U (Utility). Some important improvements were made, however: a slanted, easy-to-read instrument panel and tilted steering wheel, and a host of options, including an air precleaner, a rear exhaust, and an exhaust "silencer" for use where engine noise was objectionable.

The price gap between the 330 and the more powerful 430 was so small that the 330 sold only 1,091 units: 839 Standards and 252 Utilities. Needless to say, they are much in demand by collectors. In almost any condition, a tractor that is complete is worth more now than when it was new.

Collecting Comments

Following is a chart of the two 330 types. The star system investment rating is shown for each. Note that the two versions are intermingled in the serial number sequence.

The S was the normal height, whereas the U was low. Both had adjustable wheel spacing, front and rear.

Serial Numbers and Year Models

The following chart provides a means of determining a tractor's year model:

Year	Beginning Serial Number
1958	330001
1959	330171
1960	330935

Model 430

As with the others in the 30 Series, the 430 was the epitome of the line—the culmination of forty-four years of two-cylinder tractor experience. It was introduced, along with the others in the series, in 1958. Like the other Dubuque-built tractors that shared its heri-

Model 330 Specifications

Years produced:		1958–1960
First serial number:		330001
Last serial number:		331091
Total built:		1,091 (approx.)
Price, new:		$2,200 (1960)

	Drawbar Hp	PTO/Belt Hp
Engine		
Gasoline	22.4	24.9

General Specifications		
Engine displacement		100.5ci
Engine bore and stroke		4x4in
Engine rated rpm		1850
Tires, standard		
Rear		9-24
Front		5x15

	330S	330U
Length	115.7in	119.3in
Height to radiator	56in	50in
Weight		2,750lb
Transmission		
Speeds forward		4
Reverse		1

Rating	Model	Years	Serial Numbers	Remarks
★★★★ ★★★★★	330S 330U	1958–1960	330001–331091	4x4in engine Gasoline

tage, it used the vertical inline two-cylinder engine. It was available in the same nine basic configurations as the 40, although in both cases only seven are listed, as the T version was available with dual-tricycle, single-front-wheel, and wide-front arrangements. Listed below are the designations, or code letters, stamped on the serial number plates to indicate the type. Also listed are the number of each type built.

A 430 Row-Crop Utility tractor with a John Deere 4640 cultivator in 1958. *Deere & Company*

Model 430 Specifications				
Years produced:				1958–1960
First serial number:				140001
Last serial number:				161096
Total built:			12,680 (approx.; all types)	
Price, new:				$2,500
			Drawbar	**PTO/Belt**
Engine			**Hp**	**Hp**
Gasoline			27.1	29.2
Tractor fuel			21.9	23.5
LPG			28	30
General Specifications				
Engine displacement				113.5ci
Engine bore and stroke				4.25x4in
Engine rated rpm				1850
Tires, standard	430S	430T	420W	430H
Rear	9-24	9-24	10-24	10-38
Front	5x15	5x15	5x15	6.5x16
Length	114.8in	114.8in	119.3in	132in
Weight	2,750lb	3,000lb	3,250lb	3,400lb
Transmission				
Speeds forward				
Standard				4
Optional				5
Reverse				1
Direction Reverser				Optional

Type	Code	Number Built
Standard	S	1,795
Utility	U	1,381
Row-Crop Utility	W	5,965
Hi-Crop	H	212
Special	V	63
Tricycle (convertible)	T	3,264
Crawler	C	2,287

The 430 featured the new slanted instrument panel, with additional instruments, and the tilted steering wheel. It also sported the new, more comfortable seat and the hydraulic three-point goodies that the 320 had. Two types of fenders were optional equipment: regular and heavy-duty, which curved over the tire.

An important new option for the 430 was the Direction Reverser. This factory- or field-installed option permitted the use of any of the forward gears for backing by simply stopping the tractor and moving the lever to the left of the instrument panel. This was a

The 430Cs, such as the one shown here, are popular with maple syrup makers for opening the sugar bush trails each spring. *Deere & Company*

Model 430C Specifications

	Drawbar	PTO/Belt
Years produced:		1958–1960
First serial number:		140001
Last serial number:		161096
Total built:		2,287
Price, new:		$3,500 (1960)
Engine	**Hp**	**Hp**
Gasoline	24.1	29.7
Tractor fuel	20	24
LPG	24	30

General Specifications

Engine displacement	113.5ci
Engine bore and stroke	4.25x4in
Engine rated rpm	1850
Length	102in
Height to top of radiator	52in
Weight	4,150lb
Transmission	
Speeds forward	
Standard	4
Optional	5
Reverse	1
Direction Reverser	Optional

The Model 430 had all the features of the 330 and more. It arrived with the 30 Series as a replacement for the 20 Series, with an emphasis on more power and operator convenience and comfort. Introduced in 1958, it continued in production into 1961. The gasoline version was advertised at 27.08 drawbar hp and 29.21 belt hp. *Deere & Company*

A 430 Standard tractor with a 4110 cultivator. *Deere & Company*

Rating	Model	Years	Serial Numbers	Remarks
★★★	430S	1958–1960	140001–161096	Standard
★★★	430U			Low adjustable front
★★	430W			2-row low wide utility
★★★★★	430H			Hi-Crop, 32in clearance
★★★★★	430V			Special, 26in clearance
★★★	430T RC	1958–1960	140001–161096	Dual narrow front
★★	430T W			Adjustable wide front
★★★★	430T N			Single front wheel
★★★	430C	1958–1960	140001–161096	4- or 5-roller crawler

great boon to tractors with front end loaders, as it greatly speeded up the process of going back and forth. This unit differed from subsequent torque converter types in that it was mechanical. Shifting was done by clutching in a reversing gear. The Direction Reverser was not available with LPG or live PTO options.

Crawlers were available in either the four- or five-roller configurations. Track widths were adjustable from 36in to 46in. Track shoe widths were available from 10in to 14in and

The two-cylinder two-cycle GM diesel of the John Deere Model 435 tractor.

were offered in several configurations for various purposes, including rubber.

Collecting Comments

Following is a chart of versions of the 430 by type, serial number, and year built. The star system investment rating is shown for each type. Note that all versions are intermixed in the serial number sequence. All types used the 4.25x4in engine; gasoline, all-fuel, and LPG variations were made. Add a star for all-fuel and LPG versions, unless they are already rated five stars.

Serial Numbers and Year Models

The following chart provides a means of determining a tractor's year model:

Year	Beginning Serial Number
1958	140001
1959	142671
1960	158632

Models 435 and 440

Since the Model 435 has a two-cycle two-cylinder engine, made by GM, it is not considered a true two-cylinder by some devotees. "How can it be?" they ask. "Its exhaust note is altogether different." If the Model LA Waterloo Boy is excluded because of its horizontally opposed two-cylinder engine, so should be the 435. Both engines have evenly spaced power strokes, whereas the true two-cylinder does not, firing on a 180-degree–540-degree schedule.

Be that as it may, the 435 is a nice little tractor, and about 4,488 examples were made. They were basically the Model 430 Row-Crop Utility with 13.6-28 rear tires, 6-16 front tires, and the GM engine.

The GM diesel engine had a bore of 3.875 and a stroke of 4.5, for a displacement of 106.1ci. The compression ratio was 17:1, and the unit was supercharged. Tested at the

The Model 435, with its GM diesel, had only about one year's production run.

University of Nebraska, it produced 32.9hp at the PTO belt and 28.4hp at the drawbar at 1850rpm.

In 1958, the Farm and Industrial Equipment Institute (FIEI) and the American Society of Agricultural Engineers (ASAE), along with the Society of Automotive Engineers (SAE), set up standards for farm tractor and implement interfaces. Thus, it was ensured that implements by one manufacturer would be compatible with any tractor within the same class. Both hitches and PTOs were standardized. For the first time, the 1000rpm PTO was established. The Model 435 was the first John Deere to be offered with a 1000rpm PTO and tested by the University of Nebraska under the new standards.

Along with the 435, four related industrial tractors were built in 1959 and 1960: the Models 440ID, 440I, 440ICD, and 440IC. These were essentially the same as the 435 except for revised hood and grille sheet metal. The ICD and IC models were five-roller crawlers. The I and IC versions had the gasoline engine—a true two-cylinder—from the 430, except that it turned at 2000rpm and produced over 31hp. The ID and ICD models had the same GM two-cycle turbocharged two-cylinder diesel as the 435.

Collecting Comments

Following is a chart of versions of the 435 and 440 by type. The star system investment rating is shown for each type.

Rating	Model
★★★	435
★★★	440ID
★★★	440I
★★★★	440IC
★★★★	440ICD

Chapter 10

John Deere Models 62, L, and LA

Baby Brother

To appreciate the origins of the baby brother line of John Deere tractors, one has to consider how things were in the 1935–1937 time period. Hope was returning following four to five years of dire depression. Some thirteen tractor makers sold 161,000 tractors in 1935—still way short of the pre-Depression high of about 250,000. The John Deere B had just come on the scene, and the A was giving every indication of becoming a success. The Social Security Act had just been passed as part of the New Deal programs, and the new *Life* magazine was introduced in time to record the crash of the dirigible *Hindenburg*.

Farmers were beginning to feel some optimism. For the small farmer using one team of horses or mules for all cultivation, the step to a tractor was still a long one. Deere marketing people were not satisfied that the new smaller B was going to be able to appeal to this two-animal market. Accordingly, the Waterloo engineers began work on the even-

The Model L, left, and the Model LA were designed by Deere as utility tractors. The L was constructed from 1937 to 1946; the LA was built from 1941 to 1946. The L could pull one 12in plow, whereas the LA could pull one 16in bottom. *Deere & Company*

smaller H. Simultaneously, at the Moline Wagon Works, a second team was formed to take a look also at a two-animal tractor.

The approach taken by the John Deere Wagon Works team was unhampered by Waterloo traditions. The only concession to heritage was that the engine would be of two cylinders. In fact, the availability of the two-cylinder 8hp Novo engine more or less prompted the configuration of the baby brother prototype, the Model Y.

About twenty-four Y tractors were built and tested. In the summer of 1937, seventy-eight of an improved version, called the Model 62, were manufactured, most of which were sold to the public. Finally, for the

1937–1938 model year, the 62 was upgraded to the Model L and serious production began.

The layout of the new design was unique. The engine was slightly offset to the left, and the driver's seat to the right. The steering shaft and wheel were also offset to the left, rather than being directly in front of the driver. The engine was mounted with the crankshaft in line with the direction of travel and the cylinders vertical, instead of with a transverse crank and horizontal cylinders, as on the other Deere two-cylinders. It was also mounted quite a bit farther forward than was the Deere tradition, upon a unique dual tube frame. On the Model 62 and on, a drive shaft

The Model Y in October of 1936. The Y was the prototype for the 62, which was the forerunner of the L. *Deere & Company*

reached from the clutch back to the transmission, positioned between the driver's feet. The Y used a Model A Ford transmission mounted directly to the clutch housing with a short shaft back to the differential.

Other breaks with tradition on the baby Deere were a gasoline-only engine, a foot-operated clutch, individual rear wheel brakes with the pedals together on the right side, and a side valve (L-head) engine. Perhaps that's where the L designation came from, although the GP of 1928 also used the L-head configuration.

On the whole, the new tractor was much more "conventional"—as regarding how most tractors of the time were built—than the rest of the Deere line. It was the first of a new breed of lightweight utility tractors, such as the Allis-Chalmers B, the Massey Pony, and the Farmall A. These are the

Models 62 and L Specifications

Years produced:		1937–1946
First serial number:		621000
Last serial number:		642038
Total built:		12,500 (approx.)
Price, new:		$450 (1940), free on board (FOB) Moline

	Drawbar	PTO/Belt
Engine	**Hp**	**Hp**
3.25x4in	9.1	10.4

General Specifications

Engine displacement	
To serial number 622580	57ci
After serial number 625000	66ci
Engine rated rpm	1550
Tires, standard	
Rear	6x22
Front	4x15
Length	91in
Height to radiator	57in
Weight	1,550lb
Transmission	
Speeds forward	3
Reverse	1

The Models L and LA utility tractors were built by the John Deere Wagon Works in Moline. This is an early, styled L.

tractors much sought after today by land-scapers, mowers of large lawns, and enthusi-asts who live in the country.

Only a few of the Y prototypes used the Novo engine. Most were fitted with the 3x4in Hercules NXA engine. The Model 62 contin-ued with this engine, as did the L.

For the 1939 model year, the L received the Dreyfuss styling treatment—beginning with serial number 625000—and the Hercules NXB engine, in which the bore was increased to 3.25in. Model Ls with serial numbers 640000 and on were equipped with a Deere-made version of the Hercules engine. Parts for the Hercules were in many cases inter-changeable with those of the Deere engine. The main difference was that the Deere engine had a one-piece casting for the block and clutch housing, whereas the Hercules had a two-piece arrangement. Also, the Deere engine had provisions for a starter and generator.

Model LA Specifications

	Drawbar	PTO/Belt
Years produced:		1941–1946
First serial number:		1001
Last serial number:		13475
Total built:		12,500 (approx.)
Price, new:		$600 (1942)
Engine	**Hp**	**Hp**
3.5x4in	13.1	14.3
General Specifications		
Engine displacement		76ci
Engine rated rpm		1850
Tires, standard		
Rear		8x24
Front		5x15
Length		93in
Height to radiator		60in
Weight		2,200lb
Transmission		
Speeds forward		3
Reverse		1

The unstyled Model L differs from the prototype Model 62 in that the 62 has a JD logo below the radiator.

A late Model L with the Deere-built vertical two-cylinder engine, instead of the Hercules-built en-gine used on earlier models.

Harold Dobbratz stands proudly beside his 1937
Model L.

The right side view of Dobbratz's 1937 Model L,
serial number 621303.

Finally, the LA, produced for a time simultaneously with the L, had a Deere-built engine with a 3.5in bore. This engine was rated at 1850rpm, rather than 1550rpm, as the previous engines were. The LA was introduced for the 1941 model year. It had its own serial number sequence, beginning with 1001. The LA was equipped with a belt pulley and a 540rpm PTO, whereas earlier versions had only the belt pulley.

Collecting Comments

Following is a chart of the baby brother tractors by type, serial number, and year built. The star system investment rating is shown for each type. No original Y proto-types are known to exist, although at least one faithful re-creation has been made, by Jack Kreeger of Omaha, Nebraska.

Not many of the seventy-eight original Model 62s survive, although several are around today in pristine condition. The 62s can be distinguished from the Ls by a stylized JD in the casting under the radiator and on the rear axle housing. Other differences can be found, of course, but in general, the unstyled L and the 62 look quite a lot alike.

A 1945 Model LA, owned by Owen Bailey of Comanche, Iowa. The LA can be distinguished from the L by the noticeably larger rear wheels. Although these tractors looked small, about the same size as today's garden tractor, they were capable of serious farm work. During the early forties, many horses were still employed in routine farming, and each of these tractors was considered able to replace two teams.

The rear view of John Deere Model LI, serial number IL-501323. These tractors were favorites of highway departments as sickle-bar mower tractors.

Rating	Model	Years	Serial Numbers	Remarks
★★★★★	62	1937	621000–621078	Only 78 built 3x4in engine
★★★★★	L	1937–1938	621079–622580	Unstyled, 3x4in engine, 1,502 built
★★★	L	1938–1941	625000–634840	Styled, 3.25x4in engine
★★★★	LI	1938–1941	625000–634840	Early Industrial
★★★★	LI	1942–1946	50001–52019	Late Industrial
★★★	LA	1941–1946	1001–13475	3.5x4in engine

The styled L and the LA also look alike, unless the two types are together. Then the larger, heavier rear wheels of the LA catch the eye.

The LI tractor was basically the same as the L except it sat lower and had a wider wheel tread. The front axle was longer and the spindles shorter. The rear wheels were

The front view of a Model LI. Note the wider, lower stance.

The Model LI has a longer axle tube and a shorter kingpin tube than its nonindustrial counterparts.

The wider stance of the Model LI is facilitated in the rear by axle extensions, just inboard of the wheel.

A rare Model 62, one of only twenty-two still in existence, owned by Don Klien of Peru, Illinois.

Note the distinguishing JD logo below the radiator. The 62 was the preproduction model of the L.

moved outward with spacers. These differences, plus the LI's normally yellow paint scheme, set the LI apart from the L. Note that the LI version had its own serial number sequence beginning in 1942; before that time, examples were intermingled with the Ls.

A number of these tractors were built with Hi-Crop front axles and larger rear tires. Add a star to these, unless they already have five stars.

Serial Numbers and Year Models

The following chart provides a means of determining a tractor's year model:

Year	Beginning Serial Number	
	62 and	
	L	LA
1937	621000	
1938	621079	
1939	626265	
1940	630160	
1941	634191	1001
1942	640000	5361
1943	640738	6029
1944	641038	6159
1945	641538	9732
1946	641958	11529

The Hercules engine of the Model L can be differentiated from the Deere engine in that it has a split-line between the engine and the clutch housing.

Also, on the Deere engine, the oil filler pipe angles outward to make room for a generator; here, the pipe is vertical.

One of the several acceptable exhaust configurations available to the Model L restorer.

Chapter 11

Collection Protection

Excerpted from *Two-Cylinder* magazine

Through their power, design, and heritage, two-cylinder tractors have exerted quite a pull not only in the fields of America, but also on our heart strings. No doubt about it—vintage John Deere two-cylinders have become one of the "hot" collectibles of the 1990's.

That's the good news.

Now for the bad . . . as more people get bitten by the tractor collecting bug, as unrestored two-cylinders become more difficult to find, and especially as the antique rigs soar in value, the potential for fraud and theft also increases dramatically.

Collectors needn't be at the mercy of the unscrupulous seller or the outright thief, however. According to Craig Beek, Manager of Corporate Security for Deere & Company, two-cylinder buyers and owners who practice a few simple precautions may avoid financial loss and legal entanglements.

"Put yourself in the position of the police officer who investigates the theft of an antique tractor," suggests Beek, who cracked some of Iowa's most celebrated criminal cases during his twenty years in law enforcement and seven years as the Director of the Iowa Bureau of Criminal Investigation. "Ask yourself what information could be useful for the law enforcement investigator—especially if he doesn't know the difference between a Hi-Crop and a Model 'R'."

A two-cylinder owner can help the law enforcement investigator by providing photographs and written information that detail the stolen tractor. A close-up shot of the identification number plate (also called the "serial number plate") is essential. The picture should clearly show the tractor's identifying number, the style and spacing of numbers and letters, the shape of the plate, and any characteristics peculiar to that particular plate.

In addition, Beek urges collectors to take detailed photos of their tractors from various angles, even if the machines are still unrestored. Photograph the tractor's imperfections as well as any alterations you have made.

"Collectors should not only photograph, but record in writing all the tractor's anomalies—everything from welds to extra holes, from fender repairs to hub alterations," says Beek. "Anything that could aid in identifying the tractor as *yours* should be recorded in writing and photographs. Then file those records in a safe place, and check with your insurance agent to make sure your policy adequately covers potential losses."

If your two-cylinder is stolen, show the photographs to the investigating officer. Once an officer knows the identification number, it can be entered into the FBI's National Crime Information Center (NCIC) computer. When another officer locates your tractor, the NCIC will be contacted to determine if a machine with that identification

18 John Deere Tractors

TRACTOR satisfaction depends first of all upon selecting the type of tractor that is best adapted to your particular needs and in a power size that will handle your farm jobs most efficiently and most economically.

With general purpose tractors in five power sizes and thirteen models, standard tread tractors in three power sizes, and orchard tractors in two power sizes, John Deere offers you the most complete, most modern line of wheel-type tractors available. There's a size and type that's just right for your crops . . . your acreage . . . and your soil conditions.

And, remember, each of these 18 great tractors is built with exclusive John Deere Two-Cylinder Engine Design to give you greater simplicity, greater dependability, greater economy, and longer life.

THERE'S A SIZE AND MODEL FOR EVERY Farm, EVERY Crop, EVERY Purpose

39

The John Deere line-up for 1941 featured eighteen different models. *Deere & Company*

number has been reported as stolen. NCIC thus serves as a link between all law enforcement agencies that are involved either in reporting the theft or in locating the stolen machine.

What if your two-cylinder no longer has an identification number plate? Beek suggests collectors photograph and record any other numbers that appear to be unique to that tractor, particularly those located on the engine or transmission.

"The police could recover your stolen tractor, but the identification number plates may have been stripped off," Beek says. "Unless there's enough hard evidence to prove in court that the tractor in question does in fact belong to you, you won't get it back. Your records of unique numbers could make a big difference in proving ownership."

Beek strongly recommends that collectors take advantage of an additional identification system called the "Farm Bureau" or "Iowa" System. Under the Iowa System, owners die-stamp an owner-applied number (OAN) somewhere on the tractor. The local sheriff's office assigns and then records the number. Beek developed the system during the early 1970's while serving as the Director of the Iowa Bureau of Criminal Investigation, and it is currently used in most parts of the United States and Canada.

The Iowa System is simple but effective. The local sheriff's office assigns numbers to an individual according to a systematic numbering method. The first two "digits" are the state postal abbreviations; the next three numbers are county designations within the state; the next four are sequence numbers for that particular owner assigned by the sheriff; and the last "digit" is the first letter of the owner's last name.

"So, for instance," says Beek, "if I lived in Des Moines, Iowa, I might be assigned the owner-applied number, 'IA0771234B' to die-stamp on my two-cylinder. 'IA' stands for Iowa, '077' for Polk County, '1234' for me, and 'B' for Beek."

"You'd be amazed at how fast and how far some of these stolen tractors can travel," he continues. "It's no surprise for a tractor taken from Minnesota to be found in Texas. But with an OAN, the police officer who suspects

he's found a stolen tractor can at least pinpoint the state and county where the rightful owner lives."

The OAN should be placed anywhere on the back where it won't lessen the value of the two-cylinder. Each time a collector buys a vintage Deere, his OAN should be die-stamped beneath those of previous owners.

Although collectors can apply any identifying mark or number to their machines, Beek warns against using Social Security numbers since the Social Security Administration will not readily identify those numbers to law enforcement officials.

In an effort to help two-cylinder owners locate their stolen tractors, Deere & Company's Corporate Security Department has offered to become the central repository for information about stolen tractors. The information will be entered into Deere's internal computer system. If law enforcement officials inquire about a two-cylinder that they suspect is "hot," Beek's office will provide them with the information that the machine was in fact reported as stolen.

In addition, Deere Security Analyst Wesley Eller can aid officers in sorting out what is the correct identification number for a stolen two-cylinder. "Sometimes a tractor—especially an older model—will have digits that are both stamped and painted on a single identification plate," says Eller, who has developed sophisticated computer programs to handle Deere's complex security needs. "Owners and law enforcement officers aren't always certain what information on the plate makes up the complete identification number. In other cases, the owner or investigator may have written down only part of the identification number. Or a '2' somehow becomes a 'Z' during the course of the investigation. We've seen all kinds of ways identification numbers can get confused."

Although inquiries to Deere about stolen antique tractors have been infrequent in the past, Corporate Security has a good track record in providing law enforcement with information critical to "making a case." "In one case, the decals and identifying plates on a Model '60' had been totally obliterated after it was stolen," says Eller. "The tractor was almost impossible to identify. But by doing some investigation in our office and the Deere Archives, we were able to provide the police with the information they needed to nail down the case."

So if you open your shed doors one morning only to find your two-cylinder has disappeared, contact the law enforcement agent in your area immediately. Provide photos and written descriptions that can help identify the machine, including the tractor's model, style, date of manufacture, and unique features.

Next, insist that the agency that took the report enters the identification number of the stolen tractor into the "Vehicle File" of the FBI's NCIC computer.

Finally, make use of the liaison capabilities of Deere's Office of Corporate Security. Send a copy of the investigative report with a cover letter containing your name, address, and phone number to:

Wesley R. Eller
Corporate Security Department
Deere & Company
John Deere Road
Moline, IL 61265

The flip side of protecting yourself from theft is protecting yourself from thieves. How can you be sure that gleaming styled Model "D" you're about to buy is as old and as original as the seller insists? Again, Craig Beek has a few tips for the wise buyer.

"Whenever you buy an antique tractor, get and keep plenty of proof of the transaction," he says. "We call it, 'creating black on white'—gathering evidence that can support your claim of ownership. Sometimes deals that sound too good to be true are just that."

The watchwords when buying an antique tractor are: exercise caution and protect yourself.

If you're buying a tractor that has an identification number plate, examine it closely. Does it *look* new? Are there scratches that may be evidence of restamping? Does the letter spacing or style differ from that on other machines of the same model and year? Has the plate been attached by screws or incorrect style rivets?

Any of these characteristics should make you suspicious of a tractor's identification

plates, although they are not necessarily proof of counterfeiting or tampering.

And speaking of factory product identification numbers, Beek has a word of caution for collectors: "In most states, it's a felony, pure and simple, to alter *any* factory-installed identification number. As a matter of fact, even *possession* of a machine whose identification has been modified could subject you to legal penalties."

Beek speaks not only from years of law enforcement experience, but also as an avid collector of Ford Model T's. "Antique cars or antique tractors—there are dishonest sellers out there who'll try to make an extra buck by tampering with the machine's age and identity."

Identification plates aren't the only things altered on antique tractors to fool the unwary buyer. Beek suspects chop-shop operations exist in which parts of stolen tractors are combined and sold as original "restored" machines.

"There's nothing wrong with the legitimate restorer using parts from other tractors, as long as he documents it and tells a buyer what's original and what's not," Beek says. "If a seller represents a two-cylinder as something it's not, he's running the risk of civil liability—basically, fraud—let alone possible criminal penalties."

"These things aren't just piles of junk anymore," Beek continues. "They're expensive to buy, expensive to restore. Unfortunately, any time a lot of money is involved, there are people willing to take advantage of others."

Beek suggests buyers not only carefully examine the identification plate and the tractor itself, but also ask for documentation of prior sales, restoration, and modification. "And if I were buying a vintage tractor, I'd insist on a notarized bill of sale to certify that I'm the true owner. Although it's no guarantee that something won't go sour down the road, documenting the sale at least shows that I bought this tractor in good faith."

What if despite all your precautions and making of a "paper trail," you buy a tractor from Joe, but Joe previously stole the tractor? "Unfortunately for you, since Joe didn't have rightful ownership," says Beek, "*you* don't either. Law enforcement officials and the courts normally follow the principle that, 'a thief can pass no better title than he holds.' " Courts have upheld this principle even when the buyer didn't know the tractor had been stolen.

Not only can a buyer get swindled by thieves, but he can also be caught in the cross fire between feuding heirs. "Let's say that spoke-wheeled Model 'D' belonged to Grandpa, then Grandpa dies and Grandson sells it to you. Two years later, the rest of the grandchildren say, 'Hey! That was *our* tractor as much as Grandson's. Grandson had no right to sell it to you.' Of course," Beek adds with a chuckle, "they'll wait until *after* you've sunk a lot of time and money into restoring the 'D' before claiming it belongs to them."

In a nutshell, don't get yourself into a bind. Research, document, register, photograph, record, file, notarize, contact your insurance company, and don't tamper with dates.

Will all this caution put a chill on the friendly negotiations and warm relations created by two-cylinder deals made at swap meets and across the farmer's fence? Beek doesn't [think] so.

"Being realistic and taking precautions will just add integrity to collecting," says this owner of seven Model T's. Improved documentation can only enhance the value of two-cylinders and protect both buyers and sellers. "The key to collecting," says Beek, "is owning the genuine item—being able to say, 'This is a *real* antique John Deere.' "

"Vintage Deeres are valuable because of what they are," Wesley Eller says. "If you want to increase the value of your tractor, do it legitimately."

"We just want people to be aware of potential problems and avoid them," Beek adds. "If we can help even one two-cylinder collector avoid being cheated, we've done our job."

Sources

Tom Detweiler Sales and Service
S3266 Hwy. 13 S.
Spencer, WI 54479

Travis Jorde
935 9th Ave. NE
Rochester, MN 55904

Brandon Pfieffer
7810 Upper Mt. Vernon Rd.
Mt. Vernon, IN 47620

K. Johnson
6530 Maple Grove Rd.
Cloquet, MN 55720

The John Deere boneyard at Tom Detweiler's shop.
Detweiler deals in antique tractor parts, specializing in John Deere.

Wengers, Inc.
251 S. Race St.
Meyerstown, PA 17067

K & K Antique Tractors
R.R. 3, Box 384X
Shelbyville, IN 46176

John Herpick
R.R. 2, Box 302
Troy, KS 66087
    Specializes in Deere parts

Connecticut Yankee Tractor
Ed Bezanson
85-A Dayton Rd.
Waterford, CT 06385
    Reprinted manuals

Clarence Goodburn
R.R. 2A-P
Madelia, MN 56062
    Catalogs, manuals, and literature for all
tractors

GRATCO
Tom Franklin
2384 Deborah Ct.
Parker, CO 80134
    Assortment of literature

Jack Kreeger
7529 Beford Ave.
Omaha, NE 68134
    Deere manuals for LI and L tractors

Brian DeWitt
R.R. 1, Box 132
Nazen, ND 58545
    Specializes in Deeres

Heartland Automotive
1612 17th St.
Central City, NE 68826
    Complete restoration services; steering
wheel restoration

Wayne T. Shankle
3028 Jefferson Pike
Jefferson, MD 21775
    Specializes in new and used Deere parts

Mike McFarlane
1520 S. Elyria Rd.
Wooster, OH 44691
    Specializes in Deere parts

Craig Roy
1513 Beach St.
Salina, KS 67401
    Specializes in Deere magnetos

Wallace Gregoire, Jr.
15335 Denham Rd.
Pride, LA 70770
    Specializes in Deere parts

Red Barn Shop
6770 Kelso Rd.
Weldon, CA 93283
    Seatbacks for Deere Model M; choke and
start knobs for L, LA, A, and B

Rosewood Machine & Tool Co.
Duane Helman
Box 17
Rosewood, OH 43070
    Custom castings, manifolds for Deere

Shuck's Used Parts
Rt. 3
Lawrence, KS 66044
    Specializes in Deere 720 parts

Minn-Kota
R.R. 1, Box 99
Milbank, SD 57252
    Restoration and replacement steering
wheels

M. E. Miller
17386 State Hwy. 2
Wauseon, OH 43567
    Rare tire sizes and types, front and rear

Dean Miller
19 W. Pennsylvania Ave.
Stewartstown, PA 17363
    Specializes in Dubuque-built Deere parts

Broken Kettle Books
702 E. Madison
Fairfield, IA 52556
    Assortment of literature

Ronald E. Brungart
R.D. 2, Box 172-A
Mill Hall, PA 17751
Radiator parts for Deere Models L, LI, and LA

John Miller
Box 743
Durant, IA 52747
Deere pushrod sleeves, water plugs

Lee W. Pedersen
78 Taft Ave.
Lynbrook, NY 11563
Extensive list of parts including electrical supplies, oilers, and drain cocks as well as gas tank sealer

Otto Gas Engine Works
2167 Blue Ball Rd.
Elkton, MD 21921
Piston rings, gaskets, carburetor kits

Tim Sieren
R.R. 2, Box 180A
Keota, IA 52248
Radiator shutters for Deere Models A, B, and G

Charles Krekow
R.R. 1, Box 14
Marcus, IA 51035
Deere radiator guards

Two Cylinder Diesel Shop
Roger Marlin
R.R. 2, Box 241
Conway, MO 65632
Complete restoration services; specializes in Deere diesel tractors

Jack Law
R.R.
Pierson, IA 51048
Magneto and carburetor repair for Deeres

Jim Osborn Reproductions, Inc.
3070A Briarcliff Rd.
Atlanta, GA 30329
General source for decals

A to Z Products
P.O. Box 184-A
Malta, IL 60150
Reproduction spark plugs for Deere tractors

Seth Delaney
6171 LaFayette Rd.
Hopkinsville, KY 42240
Deere engine parts

Mike Green
2540 E. 29th St.
Des Moines, IA 50317
Specializes in gas tanks, cooling tanks, and other parts of gas engines

Hinrichs Repair
Rt. 2
Morrison, IL 61270
Two-cylinder engine rings and sleeves

Nebraska Tractor Testing Laboratory
Department of Agricultural Engineering
University of Nebraska
Lincoln, NE 68583-0832
Copies of the complete reports of tractor tests conducted by the state of Nebraska, covering most makes and models since 1919; write for a list and prices

Recommended Reading

Special-Interest Magazines
Green Magazine
R.R. 1, P.O. Box 7
Bee, NE 68314

   Green Magazine is a publication for John Deere equipment enthusiasts, featuring later products as well as those of the two-cylinder era. It is published by Richard and Carol Hain.

Two-Cylinder magazine
Two-Cylinder Club
P.O. Box 219
Grundy Center, IA 50638

   Two-Cylinder is a bimonthly magazine featuring extraordinary photography and detailed information on John Deere tractors. It's the official publication of the Two-Cylinder Club, an organization of well over twenty thousand members worldwide with dozens of local chapters that are helpful to the novice or expert collector and enthusiast.

General-Interest Magazines
Antique Power
Patrick Ertel, Editor
P.O. Box 838
Yellow Springs, OH 45387

   Antique Power is also compiling registries on Earthmaster, Friday, Leader, Sears, Sheppard, and other orphan or low-production tractors.

Belt Pulley magazine
P.O. Box 83
Nokomis, IL 62075

Engineers & Engines
1118 N. Raynor Ave.
Joliet, IL 60435

Gas Engine magazine
P.O. Box 328
Lancaster, PA 17603

Iron-Men Album
P.O. Box 328
Lancaster, PA 17603

Successful Farming
P.O. Box 4536
Des Moines, IA 50336

Books
The American Farm Tractor, by Randy Leffingwell, Motorbooks International
How to Restore Your Farm Tractor, by Robert N. Pripps, Motorbooks International
John Deere's Company, by Wayne G. Broehl, Jr., Doubleday and Company, 1984
Fordson, Farmall, and Poppin' Johnny, by Robert C. Williams, University of Illinois Press, 1987
How Johnny Popper Replaced the Horse, by Donald S. Huber and Ralph C. Hughes, Deere & Company, 1988
John Deere Tractors and Equipment, 1837–1959, vol. 1, by Don Macmillan, American Society of Agricultural Engineers
John Deere Tractors and Equipment, 1960–1990, vol. 2, by Don Macmillan, American Society of Agricultural Engineers
John Deere Tractors: Big Green Machines in Review, by Henry Rasmussen, Motorbooks International, 1987
The Agricultural Tractor 1855–1950, by R. B. Gray, American Society of Agricultural Engineers, 1954
John Deere Tractors 1918–1976, reprinted by permission of Deere & Company, American Society of Agricultural Engineers, 1987
Encyclopedia of American Farm Tractors, by C. H. Wendel, Crestline Publications

   All of the above books are available from Motorbooks International Publishers and Wholesalers Inc., PO Box 2, Osceola, WI 54020 or by calling 800-826-6600

Index